# TOUCAN'S TREE-MENDOUS
## CRAFTS FOR KIDS

Gospel Light's
SonQuest
Rainforest
VBS

INCLUDES
CD
Rom!

Gospel Light

**THIS YEAR'S RAINFOREST** theme gives each activity center the opportunity to bring to life a different and fun rainforest location. The Craft Center takes place in Toucan's Treetop and features crafts that will help kids remember their fun-filled visit to SonQuest Rainforest. Kids will get to let their creativity flow as they create crafts that will emphasize the Bible stories, Bible verses, the Daily Challenges and more! As leaders of this center, give yourself a fun camp name like Jungle Julie or Crafty Kate. Dress in explorer's clothing. Make the theme come alive for your VBS students! You'll have as much fun as the kids—maybe more!

### GOSPEL LIGHT VACATION BIBLE SCHOOL

**Senior Managing Editor,** Sheryl Haystead • **Editor,** Karen McGraw • **Contributing Writers,** Jane Eilert, Karine Masterson • **Contributing Editors,** Mary Gross Davis, Janis Halverson • **Art Director,** Lori Hamilton • **Senior Designer,** Carolyn Thomas

**Founder,** Dr. Henrietta Mears • **Publisher,** William T. Greig • **Senior Consulting Publisher,** Dr. Elmer L. Towns • **Senior Consulting Editor,** Wesley Haystead, M.S.Ed. • **Senior Editor, Theology and Biblical Content,** Dr. Gary S. Greig

# CONTENTS

# COURSE DESCRIPTION

Enter a world of amazing animals, fabulous fish, intelligent insects—we've traveled a long way upriver to discover this abundant rainforest! *SonQuest Rainforest* is far from the ordinary. It's a vibrant and dynamic place filled with enormous plants that seem to cover everything and that echoes day and night with the sounds of lively birds and animals!

With easy-to-make decorations that explode in jungle hues, your church can be transformed into a vivid rainforest environment where kids discover the sights, sounds and smells of brilliantly-colored birds, misty waterfalls, wild weather, pineapple and chocolate, and animals that seem to have come from the Garden of Eden itself! Everything your *SonQuest Rainforest* adventurers encounter is based on five parables told by Jesus that will make a difference in their lives every day. These five days of discovery not only give kids the knowledge of God's Word, but also the opportunity to respond to His truth by living out their Christian faith.

- Kids will **Get It!** As they hear the truths of the **Parable of the Sower**, kids will understand the importance of not only hearing God's Word, the Bible, but also living it out every day.

- Kids will **Get Found!** As they hear Jesus tell the **Parable of the Lost Sheep**, they'll discover what it means to be lost and how each one can be found by Jesus to become part of God's family.

- Kids will **Get God's Love!** As they listen to the **Parable of the Good Samaritan**, kids will be inspired to share God's immeasurable love with others.

- Kids will **Get Praying!** From the **Parable of the Friend at Midnight**, they'll understand the peace that comes from knowing that anytime is the right time to pray to Jesus.

- Kids will **Get Going!** As they understand the **Parable of the Talents**, they'll discover what it means to love God by doing their best.

This summer, bring your kids to *SonQuest Rainforest* VBS—an experience of discovery they'll never forget! Best of all, *SonQuest Rainforest* will take your kids beyond what they can explore with their senses to discover a living spiritual relationship with Jesus Christ, the Son of God: "For God so loved the world that he gave his one and only Son, that whoever believes in him shall not perish but have everlasting life" (John 3:16).

**Gospel Light**

# COURSE OVERVIEW

Gospel Light's
SonQuest Rainforest

## BIBLE THEME: JOHN 3:16

| DAILY CHALLENGE | BIBLE STORY DISCOVERY | LIFE DISCOVERY | BIBLE VERSE DISCOVERY |
|---|---|---|---|
| **Get It!** 1 | **Which Soil Are You?** Matthew 13:1-23; Mark 4:1-20; Luke 8:4-15 | When we believe God's Word, it gives us the guidance we need to know how to live. | "I have hidden your word in my heart that I might not sin against you." Psalm 119:11 |
| **Get Found!** 2 | **Baa, Baa, Lost Sheep** Matthew 18:12-14; Luke 15:3-7; Luke 23 | Jesus' death and resurrection make it possible for each person to experience God's love forever. | "For God so loved the world that he gave his one and only Son, that whoever believes in him shall not perish but have eternal life." John 3:16 |
| **Get God's Love!** 3 | **An Unlikely Neighbor** Luke 10:25-37 | God's love is so amazing that it motivates us to love Him in return and pass His love on to others. | "Love the Lord your God with all your heart and with all your soul and with all your mind. . . . Love your neighbor as yourself." Matthew 22:37-39 |
| **Get Praying!** 4 | **The Midnight Knocker** Luke 11:1-13 | No matter what circumstances we are in, we can pray to God and He will hear our prayers and help us experience His goodness. | "Do not be anxious about anything, but in everything, by prayer and petition, with thanksgiving, present your requests to God. And the peace of God . . . will guard your hearts and your minds in Christ Jesus." Philippians 4:6-7 |
| **Get Going!** 5 | **Use It or Lose It** Matthew 25:14-30 | God has made us in wonderful ways so that we can love Him by serving others. | "Whatever you do, work at it with all your heart, as working for the Lord, not for men." Colossians 3:23 |

# CRAFT LEADER'S GUIDE

## Rainforest Fun!

Going on a rainforest adventure means exploring nature, building friendships, learning new skills and creating exciting memories. Children of all ages love the adventure of the rainforest! The parables of Jesus and the breathtaking atmosphere of SonQuest Rainforest inspired the crafts found in this resource book. We hope that you and your children enjoy many fun-filled hours creating projects from *Toucan's Tree-mendous Crafts for Kids*.

## Personalize It!

Feel free to alter the craft materials and instructions in this book to suit your children's needs. Consider what materials you have on hand, what materials are available in your area and what materials you can afford to purchase. In some cases, you may be able to substitute materials you already have for the suggested craft supplies.

In addition, don't feel confined to the crafts in a particular age-level section. You may want to adapt a craft for younger or older children by using the simplification or enrichment ideas where provided.

## Three Keys for Crafting with Children

How can you make craft time successful and fun for your children? First, encourage creativity in each child! Remember, the process of creating is more important than the final product. Provide a variety of materials with which children may work. Allow children to make choices on their own. Don't insist that children "stay inside the lines."

Second, choose projects that are appropriate for the skill level of your children. Children can become discouraged when a project is too difficult for them. Finding the right projects for your children will increase the likelihood that they will be successful and satisfied with their finished products.

Finally, show an interest in the unique way each child approaches a project. Affirm the choices he or she has made. Treat each child's final product as a masterpiece!

The comments you give a child today can affect the way he or she views art in the future, so be positive! Being creative is part of being made in the image of God, the ultimate creator!

## CRAFT SYMBOLS

Many of the craft projects in *Toucan's Tree-mendous Crafts for Kids* are appropriate for more than one age level. Next to the title of certain projects, you'll find the symbol shown below. This symbol tells which projects are suitable or adaptable for all elementary-age children—first through sixth grades. As you select projects, consider the particular children you are working with. Feel free to use your own ideas to make projects simpler or more challenging, depending on the needs of your children.

In addition, some craft projects in this book require less preparation than others. The symbol shown at right tells which projects require minimal preparation.

suitable for all ages    minimal preparation

## CRAFTS WITH A MESSAGE

Many projects in *Toucan's Tree-mendous Crafts for Kids* can easily become crafts with a message. Have children create slogans or add the Daily Challenges as part of their projects; or provide photocopies of an appropriate thought or Bible verse for children to attach to their crafts. Below are some examples of ways to use messages to enhance the craft projects in this book.

## CONVERSATION

Each craft in this book includes a Conversation section designed to help you enhance craft times with thought-provoking conversation that is age appropriate. The Conversation section for a project may relate to prayer, a Scripture verse or a Bible story. Often Conversation sections will include interesting facts. If your craft program includes large groups of children, share these Conversation suggestions with each helper, who can use them with individuals or small groups.

## BE PREPARED

### If you are planning to use crafts with a child at home, here are some helpful tips:

- Focus on crafts designed for your child's age, but don't ignore projects for older or younger ages. Elementary-age children enjoy many of the projects geared for preschool and kinder-garten children. And younger children are always interested in doing "big kid" things. Just plan on working along with your child, helping with tasks he or she can't handle alone.

- Start with projects that call for materials you have around the house. Make a list of items you do not have, and plan to gather them in one expedition.

- If certain materials seem too difficult to obtain, a little thought can usually lead to appropriate substitutions. Often your creative twist ends up being an improvement over the original plan.

### If you are planning to lead a group of children in doing craft projects, keep these hints in mind:

- Choose projects that allow children to work with a variety of materials.

- Make your project selections far enough in advance to allow time to gather all needed supplies.

- Make a sample of each project to be sure the directions are fully understood and potential problems can be avoided. **You may want to adapt some projects by simplifying proce-dures or varying the materials.**

- Items can often be acquired as donations from people or busi-nesses if you plan ahead and make your needs known. Many churches distribute lists of needed materials to their congrega-tions. Some items can be brought by the children themselves.

- In making your supply list, distinguish between items that each individual child will need and those that will be shared among a group.

- Keep in mind that some materials may be shared among more than one age level. To avoid frustration, coordinate with other groups that might be using the same supplies you need so that children can complete their craft projects. Basic supplies that are used in many projects, such as glue, scissors, markers, etc., should be available in every craft room.

## HELPFUL HINTS

### Using Glue with Young Children

Because preschoolers have difficulty using glue bottles effectively, you may want to try one of the following procedures. Purchase glue in large containers (up to one gallon size).

1. Pour small amounts of glue into several margarine tubs.

2. Dilute glue by mixing a little water into each container.

3. Children use paintbrushes to spread glue on their projects.

4. When project is completed, place lids on margarine tubs to save glue for future projects.

### OR

1. Pour small amounts of glue into several margarine tubs.

2. Give each child a cotton swab.

3. Children dip cotton swabs into the glue and rub glue on projects.

4. When project is completed, place lids on margarine tubs to save glue for future projects.

### Cutting with Scissors

When cutting with scissors is required for crafts, remember that some children in your class may be left-handed. It is very difficult for a left-handed person to cut with right-handed scissors. Have available two or three pairs of left-handed scissors. These can be obtained from a school-supply center.

If your craft involves cutting fabric, felt or ribbon, have available several pairs of fabric scissors for older children.

### Using Acrylic Paints

Acrylic paints are required for several projects. Our suggestions:

- Provide smocks or old shirts for your children to wear, as acrylics may stain clothes.

- Acrylics can be expensive for a large group of children. To make paint go further, dilute it with a small amount of water. Or, use house paints thinned with water.

- Fill shallow containers with soapy water. Clean paint-brushes before switching colors and immediately after finishing project.

## CRAFT CENTER BASICS

If you'll be leading crafts at SonQuest Rainforest Vacation Bible School, *Toucan's Tree-mendous Crafts for Kids* contains more than enough crafts for each age level. For additional hints about leading a group of children in craft projects, see "Be Prepared" on page 7.

The projects in this book can be done in individual classrooms or in a Craft Center. Here's how a Craft Center works:

- Select projects that will appeal to several age levels. (Sometimes you'll find one project that all children will enjoy making. Other times you'll need to select one project for the younger children and one for the older children.)

- Recruit adults and/or youths to prepare for and run the Craft Center.

- Decorate your center with samples of crafts your kids will be making.

- As classes visit the Craft Center, lead them in making projects, tailoring instructions and conversation to the children's age level.

## STEPS TO SUCCESS

As Craft Coordinator, you play a key role in determining the quality of your craft program. Here are four crucial steps in achieving success at your task:

1. Plan ahead. Familiarize yourself with each day's craft project and plan any necessary changes.

2. Be well organized (see "SonQuest Rainforest Checklist").

3. Secure your supplies in advance. Prepare a bulletin notice listing items you need donated from members of your congregation. Also, people are often happy to help if you personally ask them to donate or purchase specific items.

4. Communicate with everyone involved. People who do not know what to do may not ask for help.

## SONQUEST RAINFOREST CHECKLIST

**16 weeks before:**

1. List all staff needs. (Determine if crafts will be led by regular teachers or by special craft leaders and if students from the Youth Department will serve as craft helpers.)

2. Meet with the VBS Director to compile a list of prospective staff.

3. Begin personal contacts to recruit needed staff.

**12 weeks before:**

1. Select projects from this book and list needed supplies.

2. Determine which items are already on hand and which need to be secured.

**8 weeks before:**

1. Distribute a bulletin notice listing needed supplies.

2. Begin organizing supplies as they are acquired. Separate inventories for each age group are often helpful, especially in large programs.

**6 weeks before:**

1. Review staffing needs with the VBS Director and plan involvement in training session.

2. Assign leaders to make a sample of each craft project that they will teach to children.

3. Distribute second notice regarding supplies.

**Tip:** Plan VBS craft preparation days. Have one or two during the day and at least one in the evening so that more volunteers can participate and be a part of VBS.

**4 weeks before:**

1. Participate in training session, showing samples of at least the first-day craft projects.

2. Distribute third notice regarding supplies.

3. Make any needed personal contacts to gather required supplies.

**2 weeks before:**

1. Purchase any supplies still needed. Adjust supplies as needed.

**During VBS:**

1. Make sure needed supplies are available for staff.

2. Secure additional supplies as needed.

# LEaDING a CHILD TO CHRIST

One of the greatest privileges of serving in VBS is helping children become members of God's family. Pray for the children you teach and ask God to prepare them to understand and receive the good news about Jesus. Ask God to give you the sensitivity and wisdom you need to communicate effectively and to be aware of opportunities that occur naturally.

Because children are easily influenced to follow the group, be cautious about asking for group decisions. Offer opportunities to talk and pray individually with any child who expresses interest in becoming a member of God's family—but without pressure. A good way to guard against coercing a child to respond is to simply ask, "Would you like to hear more about this now or at another time?"

When talking about salvation with children, use words and phrases they understand; never assume they understand a concept just because they can repeat certain words. Avoid symbolic terms ("born again," "ask Jesus to come into your heart," "open your heart," etc.) that will confuse these literal-minded thinkers. (You may also use the evangelism booklet *God Loves You!* available from Gospel Light.)

1. God wants you to become His child. Why do you think He wants you in His family? (See 1 John 3:1.)

2. You and I and every person in the world has done wrong things. The Bible word for doing wrong is "sin." What do you think should happen to us when we sin? (See Romans 6:23.)

3. God loves you so much that He sent His Son to die on the cross to take the punishment for your sin. Because Jesus never sinned, He is the only One who can take the punishment for your sin. On the third day after Jesus died, God brought Him back to life. (See 1 Corinthians 15:3-4; 1 John 4:14.)

4. Are you sorry for your sin? Tell God that you are. Do you believe Jesus died for your sin and then rose again? Tell Him that, too. If you tell God you are sorry for your sin and believe that Jesus died to take your sin away, God forgives you. (See 1 John 1:9.)

5. The Bible says that when you believe that Jesus is God's Son and that He is alive today, you receive God's gift of eternal life. This gift makes you a child of God. This means God is with you now and forever. (See John 1:12; 3:16.)

There is great value in encouraging a child to think and pray about what you have said before responding. Encourage the child who makes a decision to become a Christian to tell his or her parents. Give your pastor and the child's Sunday School teacher(s) his or her name. A child's initial response to Jesus is just the beginning of a lifelong process of growing in the faith, so children who make decisions need to be followed up to help them grow. The discipling booklet *Growing as God's Child* (available from Gospel Light) is an effective tool to use.

# aGe-LeVeL characTeRisTics

## AGES 3 TO 6

Preschool and kindergarten crafts have been planned for children who are three to six years old with a ratio of one teacher for every 4 to 6 children. Each craft provides enough flexibility so that young children can work successfully. Effectively instructing children of varying ages requires a teacher to recognize and accept wide individual differences in skills, abilities and interests. Regardless of the level at which a child works, a teacher can use the child's interest in the activity to guide his or her thinking toward understanding a Bible truth.

THREES and FOURS are just beginning to use art supplies and often find the finished product of little interest. Encourage them to try new things, but don't expect beauty or design.

KINDERGARTNERS enjoy exploring the use of art materials but may find the process tedious after a short while. To sustain their interest, offer encouragement and assistance as needed.

## GRADES 1 AND 2

The term "perpetual motion" may be used to describe children this age. Small-muscle coordination is still developing and improving. Girls are ahead of boys at this stage of development.

Children are concerned with pleasing their leaders. Each child is also struggling to become socially acceptable to the peer group. The Golden Rule is a tough concept at this age. Being first and winning are very important. Taking turns is hard, but this skill improves by the end of the second grade. A child's social process moves gradually from I to you and we.

Provide opportunities for children to practice taking turns. Help each child accept the opinions and wishes of others and consider the welfare of the group as well as his or her own welfare. Call attention to times when the group cooperated successfully.

Children are experiencing new and frequently intense feelings as they grow in independence. Sometimes the child finds it hard to control his or her behavior. There is still a deep need for approval from adults and a growing need for approval by peers.

Seek opportunities to help each child in your group KNOW and FEEL you love him or her. Show genuine interest in each child and his or her activities and accomplishments. Learn children's names and use them frequently in positive ways.

## GRADES 3 AND 4

Children at this level have good large- and small-muscle coordination. The girls are generally ahead of the boys. Children can work diligently for longer periods but can become impatient with delays or their own imperfect abilities.

Children's desire for status within the peer group becomes more intense. Most children remain shy with strangers and exhibit strong preferences for being with a few close friends. Some children still lack essential social skills needed to make and retain friendships.

Look for the child who needs a friend. Move near that child and include him or her in what you are doing.

This is the age of teasing, nicknames, criticism and increased verbal skills to vent anger. By eight years of age, children have developed a sense of fair play and a value system of right and wrong. At nine years of age, children are searching for identity beyond membership in the family unit.

You have a great opportunity to be a Christian example at a time when children are eagerly searching for models! Encourage children's creativity and boost their self-concept. Let children know by your words and by your actions that "love is spoken here" and that you will not let others hurt them or let them hurt others.

## GRADES 5 AND 6

Children have mastered most basic physical skills, are active and curious, and seek a variety of new experiences. Rapid growth can cause some 11-year-olds to tire easily. Oftentimes in coed groups, boys tend to be less aggressive and girls tend to be friendlier. The mixture seems to bring out the best in both genders.

Friendships and activities with their peers flourish. Children draw together and away from adults in the desire for independence. The child wants to be a part of a same-gender group and usually does not want to stand alone in competition.

Children are usually cooperative, easygoing, content, friendly and agreeable. Be aware that often 11-year-old children are experiencing unsteady emotions and can quickly shift from one mood to another.

Be patient with changes of feelings. Give many opportunities to make choices with only a few necessary limits. Take time to listen as students share their experiences and problems with you.

Children of this age are verbal! Making ethical decisions becomes a challenging task. They are able to express ideas and feelings in a creative way. By 11 years old, children have begun to be able to reason abstractly. They begin to think of themselves as grown-up and at the same time question adult concepts. Hero worship is strong.

Include lots of opportunities for talking, questioning and discussing in a safe, accepting environment. Ask children for their ideas of how things could be done better.

# DECORATING YOUR CRAFT CENTER

## TOUCAN'S TREETOP

Turn your Craft Center into Toucan's Treetop!
Complete instructions and patterns are available in *Rainforest Décor & More*.

# Get It!

# WHICH SOIL ARE YOU?

## BIBLE STORY DISCOVERY

Matthew 13:1-23; Mark 4:1-20; Luke 8:4-15

## BIBLE VERSE DISCOVERY

*I have hidden your word in my heart that I might not sin against you.* Psalm 119:11

## LIFE DISCOVERY

When we believe God's Word, it gives us the guidance we need to know how to live.

## DISCOVERY GOALS

During this session, each student may

1. COMPARE the four soils Jesus described;
2. DESCRIBE what it means to believe God's Word;
3. PRAY, thanking God for His Word and asking His help in obeying it;
4. CHOOSE to receive God's forgiveness and to become a member of God's family, as the Holy Spirit leads.

## BIBLE STORY RECAP

Jesus tells the story of a farmer, sowing seeds in his field. The seeds fell on four types of soil: hard soil, rocky soil, thorny soil and good soil. Only the seeds that fell on the good soil were able to produce fruit.

Jesus explained that God is like the farmer, His Word is the seed and we are like the different types of soil. People like the hard-packed soil never listen to God's Word. Those like the rocky soil happily receive God's Word, but when it becomes too hard to obey, they don't even try. Others are like the thorny soil and are happy to hear God's Word, but soon become too distracted by the busyness and worries of life to ever grow well in what they learn from the Bible.

But some people are like the good soil. They believe God's Word and every day do their best to follow it every day. These people grow and mature as Christians and bear lots and lots of good fruit.

## TEACHER'S DISCOVERY

Jesus taught the multitudes in parables. His parables used a common everyday activity or object to explain a truth of spiritual, eternal significance. But when it came to understanding the spiritual truths Jesus was teaching, many listeners just didn't **Get It!** The Parable of the Sower illustrates this.

As you read the Parable of the Sower, consider yourself: What spiritual fruit is growing in your "dirt"? As God's Word is sown in your heart, do you **Get It** readily, experiencing growth and producing fruit? Or does your heart seem hard, rocky or thorny? To help us keep our growth from being hindered, we need to always ask the Lord to prepare our hearts to receive His Word. Part of this preparation involves dealing with the "rocks and thorns" in our hearts that keep us from understanding God's Word. Take time today to ask and seek forgiveness and to invite God's Spirit to help you line up your priorities with His.

The children at SonQuest Rainforest VBS also need the soil of their hearts to be prepared to embrace God's Word. Pray, asking God to prepare the hearts of the children coming to SonQuest Rainforest VBS so that they will **Get It!** Then together, you and they will experience the beauty of God's Word, discovering the guidance you need to help you live and grow as God designed.

## DAILY DISCOVERY

At the end of each session, take time to reflect on what happened. Use these questions as a guide.

- Considering that this was the first day, what worked well?
- What should you do differently tomorrow?
- What additional resources or help will you need to make tomorrow a success?

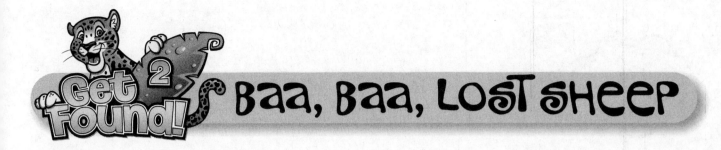

# BAA, BAA, LOST SHEEP

## BIBLE STORY DISCOVERY

Matthew 18:12-14; Luke 15:3-7; Luke 23

## BIBLE VERSE DISCOVERY

*For God so loved the world that he gave his one and only Son, that whoever believes in him shall not perish but have eternal life.* John 3:16

## LIFE DISCOVERY

Jesus' death and resurrection make it possible for each person to experience God's love forever.

## DISCOVERY GOALS

During this session, each student may

1. COMPARE ways that God is like the shepherd and each of us is like the lost sheep;

2. DISCUSS ways God shows His love;

3. PRAY, thanking God for sending Jesus to be our Savior so that we can experience His love forever;

4. CHOOSE to receive God's forgiveness and to become a member of God's family, as the Holy Spirit leads.

## BIBLE STORY RECAP

Wherever Jesus went, crowds would come to listen to Him teach about God and God's love. Some of the religious leaders didn't approve of the way Jesus allowed tax collectors and known sinners to be amongst His followers.

Jesus knew how these religious leaders felt. In order to teach them how God felt about sinners, He told the story of a shepherd who had 100 sheep. One day, after a long day of caring for his sheep, the shepherd counted them. But there were only 99 sheep! So the shepherd went and searched until he found that one lost sheep. That one sheep was important to him!

Jesus explained that God is like the shepherd and we are like the sheep. God's desire is that none of us would be lost. He will seek out and search for even one lost sheep for we are all important to Him.

## TEACHER'S DISCOVERY

The Pharisees and teachers of God's law were judging Jesus for His practice of welcoming sinners and sharing meals with them. These very devout and upright people didn't understand that they were sinners, too.

So Jesus told the story of the shepherd who leaves the ninety-nine sheep in the open, to find the one lost sheep. This story clearly made the point that God is delighted when He can bring home any "sheep" that is lost. Each one matters to Him. We ALL are lost and need to **Get Found!** Recognizing that we are lost is a first step in receiving salvation. Understanding that we cannot rescue ourselves, but need to **Get Found** is the next step. Jesus' story illustrates the extent of God's love for us, reaching into our confusion and need to bring us to Himself. Thank God for all He has done in seeking you out to save you.

Ask God to continue working in the hearts of the children at SonQuest Rainforest VBS, showing them they are like the lost sheep that need to **Get Found!** Just as that shepherd showed love and care for the one lost sheep, even when he had 99 others, Jesus truly loves and cares for each one of them!

## DAILY DISCOVERY

- What went well today? How can you translate that success into your plans for tomorrow?

- List two specific ways you can share the seeking love of Jesus with your students tomorrow.

- Praise Jesus for the students who **(Got) Found** by recognizing they are like the lost sheep and have accepted Jesus' love for them.

- Plan a way to help these children be discipled.

# an UNLiKeLY NeiGHBoR

## BiBLe StoRY DiscoveRY

Luke 10:25-37

## BiBLe VeRSe DiscoveRY

*Love the Lord your God with all your heart and with all your soul and with all your mind. . . . Love your neighbor as yourself.* Matthew 22:37-39

## LiFe DiscoveRY

God's love is so amazing that it motivates us to love Him in return and pass His love on to others.

## DiscoveRY GoaLS

During this session, each student may

1. COMPARE the actions of the people in Jesus' story of the Good Samaritan;

2. DISCUSS how we can be like the Good Samaritan who helped someone in need;

3. PRAY, thanking God for His amazing love and asking for His help to show love to Him and to others;

4. CHOOSE to receive God's forgiveness and to become a member of God's family, as the Holy Spirit leads.

## BiBLe StoRY Recap

One day Jesus was talking to a man about God's command to love your neighbor as yourself. "Who is my neighbor?" the man asked. To answer, Jesus told the Parable of the Good Samaritan.

A Jewish man traveling to Jericho was beaten and robbed. As he lay on the dirt road, a priest and a Levite both walked by, but offered no help. Then a Samaritan came down the road with his donkey. The Jewish man had no reason to expect help from the Samaritan because the Jewish and Samaritan people didn't like each other. But despite their differences, it was the Samaritan who stopped his journey, bandaged this Jewish stranger's wounds and took him on his donkey to an inn and paid for his care.

Jesus told this story to illustrate the point that EVERYONE is our neighbor. God wants us to be kind and loving to everyone, even when it isn't easy. Because God has shown amazing love to us, we can in turn show His love to others.

## TeacHeR'S DiscoveRY

"Love the Lord your God with all your heart and with all your soul and with all your mind . . . Love your neighbor as yourself" (Matthew 22:37-39). Simple to say, but is it possible to do? To love God and others in the way Jesus described is far beyond the ability of our independent natures. We are most often too selfish to fully love God and other people. Jesus is the only one who loves completely; it's only when He works in us that we can approach even a slight semblance to such a measure of love.

This week you have practiced a little of that love! How hard has this week been so far? Selflessly giving of yourself to love Jesus and others can be draining! But take some time today to evaluate what you've given along with how much Jesus is returning back to you. What have you seen kids doing? Heard them saying? Even if you come home needing a shower and a nap, it's worth it! When we love God and others with our all, we **Get God's Love!** Praise Jesus for allowing you the opportunity to love Him and others at SonQuest Rainforest VBS.

## DaiLY DiscoveRY

- Name the students you made a personal connection with today.

- Which of these students is new to your church? What can you do to help them feel at home?

- Name the students you will need to be more intentional to connect with tomorrow.

- What worked well today? What will you do differently tomorrow?

# Get Praying!
# THE MIDNIGHT KNOCKER

## BIBLE STORY DISCOVERY

Luke 11:1-13

## BIBLE VERSE DISCOVERY

*Do not be anxious about anything, but in everything, by prayer and petition, with thanksgiving, present your requests to God. And the peace of God . . . will guard your hearts and your minds in Christ Jesus.* Philippians 4:6-7

## LIFE DISCOVERY

No matter what circumstances we are in, we can pray to God and He will hear our prayers and help us experience His goodness.

## DISCOVERY GOALS

During this session, each student may

1. COMPARE the way we pray to the way Jesus taught us to pray;
2. DISCUSS reasons to trust God and pray to Him;
3. PRAY to God about our requests and thank God for answering our prayers in the very best way;
4. CHOOSE to receive God's forgiveness and to become a member of God's family, as the Holy Spirit leads.

## BIBLE STORY RECAP

To teach His disciples to pray, Jesus taught through example and parable. First, He prayed the Lord's Prayer as an example of how to pray. Then he told a story of two neighbors.

One of the men had a friend arrive for a visit late at night. The visitor was hungry. But his friend had no food! So the friend went to his neighbor's house and knocked on his door. The neighbor was already in bed and didn't want to disturb his family to unlock the door. But the friend was persistent. He continued knocking until his neighbor gave him bread to feed his visitor.

Jesus explained that God is far more willing to give us what we need than the reluctant neighbor was. Jesus also compared God to a father who, when his son asks for a fish, gives him a fish and not a snake. A father who gives his son an egg when requested, not a scorpion. Jesus wants us to know that God is better than the very BEST father on Earth!

## TEACHER'S DISCOVERY

When a doctor gives you a prescription, do you fill it and then take the medicine? Obviously, it would be foolish not to do so. Yet, God's Word gives us the prescription for peace, but too often we fail to "take it." God's prescription? Prayer—spending time communicating with God. God's Word tells us to pray continually and to pray about everything. When we follow this prescription, He offers peace that passes understanding (see Philippians 4:6-7). We are also reminded to "present our requests with thanksgiving." It has been said that thoughts of gratitude and thoughts of worry cannot both be in our minds at the same time. Thankfulness overrules worry every time!

What is troubling you? Quiet your heart and begin to praise God for things you are thankful for, even in the midst of that troubling situation. Pray and thank God for each child you know at SonQuest Rainforest VBS. You may not know the troubles they leave behind each morning, but God does; ask Him to meet their needs today. Ask God to fill your words and actions with His love for these children He has placed in your care. Be persistent in communicating with God. God's Word shows us it is always time to **Get Praying!**

## DAILY DISCOVERY

- Praise God for what worked well today.
- Ask for wisdom and energy to make tomorrow even better.
- Thank God for the opportunity to share His love with the students at SonQuest Rainforest VBS.

# USE IT OR LOSE IT

## BIBLE STORY DISCOVERY

Matthew 25:14-30

## BIBLE VERSE DISCOVERY

*Whatever you do, work at it with all your heart, as working for the Lord, not for men.* Colossians 3:23

## LIFE DISCOVERY

God has made us in wonderful ways so that we can love Him by serving others.

## DISCOVERY GOALS

During this session, each student may

1. COMPARE the feelings and actions of the workers in Jesus' story of the talents;

2. DISCUSS ways we can invest our abilities and gifts to love God by serving others;

3. PRAY, asking God for strength to work hard and invest our abilities in ways that please Him;

4. CHOOSE to receive God's forgiveness and to become a member of God's family, as the Holy Spirit leads.

## BIBLE STORY RECAP

In Jesus' Parable of the Talents, a rich man is about to go on a long journey. Before he leaves, he entrusts some of his money to three of his servants. According to what he knows about each man, the master gives a different amount of money to each. To one servant, he entrusts five talents. To another two talents are given and to the third, the master gives one talent.

The servants who received five and two talents both put the money to good work and over time, each one doubled the money they had been given. The third servant dug a hole in the ground and buried the money. He did nothing to invest that with which he had been entrusted. When the master returned, the servants who had worked hard were richly rewarded, while the third servant was sent away.

Jesus told this story because God is like the master. And to each of us, He gives different talents and abilities. Like the servants who had received five and two talents, God wants us to make the most of what we have been given. Doing so, we show how much we love our amazing God.

## TEACHER'S DISCOVERY

The Bible lesson for today reminds us to **Get Going** by making the most of every opportunity. This last day of VBS gives you a few brief hours—your last opportunity to share Jesus' love with this group of children. Reflect on the opportunities Jesus has given you this week. Thank Him for giving you opportunities according to your abilities (see Matthew 25:15). It is good to realize that God already knows our strengths and weaknesses when He calls us to do a job!

As Jesus' servant, you may have felt inadequate or ill-prepared for some tasks you were given at SonQuest Rainforest VBS. Remember that Jesus' response to your service is not based on your performance but on your faithfulness. The greatest words we will hear from Jesus are, "Well done, my good and faithful servant! Come and share in your master's happiness" (see Matthew 25:21).

Look at today's memory verse. Colossians 3:23 says, "Whatever you do, work at it with all your heart, as working for the Lord." Ask the Lord to give you eyes to see every task of the day as an assignment from Him. This perspective on your own work will help you **Get Going!** No matter where you are serving at SonQuest Rainforest VBS, always remember: "It is the Lord Christ you are serving" (Colossians 3:24). So, what are you waiting for? **Get Going**, faithful servant!

## DAILY DISCOVERY

- Praise God for the great week. Praise Him for the challenges as well as the accomplishments.

- Celebrate all He has done in the lives of the children and in your own life as well.

- Plan a way you will follow up with the children in your group.

- Commit to **Get Going** by continuing doing all your tasks for Him!

# SECTION ONE/PRESCHOOL-KINDERGARTEN
# CRAFTS FOR YOUNG CHILDREN

Craft projects for young children are a blend of "I wanna do it myself!" and "I need help!" Crafts usually require a certain amount of adult assistance—preparing a pattern, doing some cutting, preselecting magazine pictures, tying a knot, etc. But always take care to avoid robbing the child of the satisfaction of his or her own unique efforts. Do only what is absolutely necessary! The adult's desire to have a nice finished project should not override the child's pleasure in experimenting with color, shape, line and texture. Avoid the temptation to do the project for the child or to improve on his or her efforts.

Some of these crafts have enrichment and simplification ideas. An enrichment idea provides a way to make the craft more challenging for the older child. A simplification idea helps the younger child complete the craft successfully.

Although most projects in this book allow plenty of leeway for children to be creative, some children may become frustrated with the limitations of a structured craft. This frustration may be a signal that the child needs an opportunity to work with more basic, less structured materials: blank paper and markers, play dough, or precut magazine pictures to make into a collage. In any task a young child undertakes, remember that *the process the child goes through is more important than the finished product.*

17

# DiRT BUDDY (15-30 MINUTES)

## MATERIALS

- Clothing Patterns (p. 19)
- Dirt Buddy Care Instructions (p. 20)
- light-colored pantyhose or knee-highs
- permanent markers
- potting soil
- grass seed
- 10-oz. plastic cups
- variety of construction paper
- markers

**For each child—**
- 3 craft sticks

**For each helper—**
- 2 containers (storage bin, medium mixing bowl, etc.)
- tablespoon

## STANDARD SUPPLIES

- newspaper
- scissors
- craft glue

## PREPARATION

Cover tables with newspapers. If not using knee-highs, cut pantyhose into 10- to 12-inch (25.5- to 30.5-cm) pieces and tie a knot in one end of each piece. Use permanent markers to draw a simple face on each piece of pantyhose or knee high (see sketch b). Pour some grass seed into half the small containers. Pour potting soil into the remaining containers. Place craft sticks and rubber bands on tables. On construction paper, photocopy Buddy Patterns and cut out, making clothing in a variety of colors. For each child, make a copy of "Dirt Buddy Care Instructions."

## INSTRUCT EACH CHILD IN THE FOLLOWING PROCEDURES:

- Open the piece of pantyhose or knee high as wide as possible as an adult helper spoons one tablespoon of grass seed and 10-12 tablespoons of potting soil (sketch a). Count each spoonful aloud.
- Dirt Buddy should be about the size of a baseball. Press on soil to shape it as needed. Tie the pantyhose or knee high into a knot as close to the soil as possible, leaving the "tail" attached (sketch b).
- To form head support for Dirt Buddy, lay three craft sticks in the shape of a triangle. Glue the ends together (sketch c). Lay this triangle on the rim of the cup and rest the "Buddy" on top, with its "tail" hanging down through the support into the cup.
- Choose construction-paper clothing, a shirt and shorts or a skirt. Use markers to decorate clothing. Glue clothing to cup.
- Wash your hands. Get a copy of Dirt Buddy Care Instructions to take home with your Dirt Buddy.

### Simplification Ideas
- Let Dirt Buddy's head rest directly on the rim of the cup, instead of making the triangular base.

### Enrichment Ideas
- Helpers hold the piece of pantyhose or knee high while children spoon in the seeds and soil.
- Instead of construction-paper shapes, use adhesive-backed craft foam.
- Instead of drawing faces on pantyhose or knee highs before class, children make craft-foam faces. Cut a 2-inch (5-cm) circle for each child, or allow older children to cut their own shapes. Children can decorate their foam faces with markers or by gluing on additional foam shapes. Attach the foam faces with straight pins pushed into the Dirt Buddy.

## CONVERSATION

We're going to take our Dirt Buddies home and water them. In about 10 days, the seeds will sprout, grass will grow and our buddies will have grass for hair! Our Dirt Buddies will remind us of today's Bible story when Jesus said that God's Word, the Bible, is like seed thrown into a field by a farmer. Some of the farmer's seed fell on a hard path, some fell in the thorns, and some fell on the rocky soil. These seeds didn't grow. But the seeds that fell on GOOD soil grew and grew! We are like the good soil when we listen to and obey God's Word. When we do, we Get It!

a.

b.

c.

# CLOTHING PATTERNS

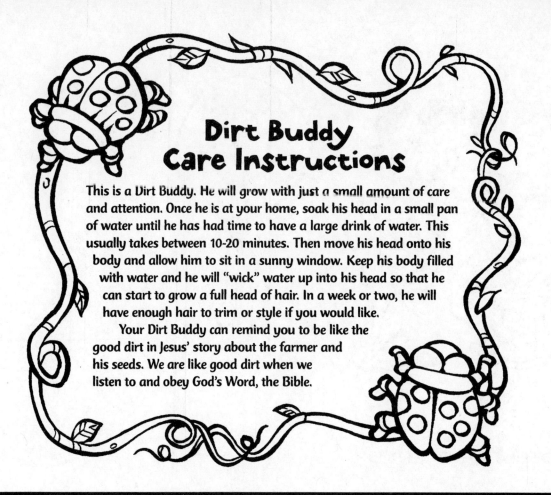

# Dirt Buddy
# Care Instructions

This is a Dirt Buddy. He will grow with just a small amount of care and attention. Once he is at your home, soak his head in a small pan of water until he has had time to have a large drink of water. This usually takes between 10-20 minutes. Then move his head onto his body and allow him to sit in a sunny window. Keep his body filled with water and he will "wick" water up into his head so that he can start to grow a full head of hair. In a week or two, he will have enough hair to trim or style if you would like.

Your Dirt Buddy can remind you to be like the good dirt in Jesus' story about the farmer and his seeds. We are like good dirt when we listen to and obey God's Word, the Bible.

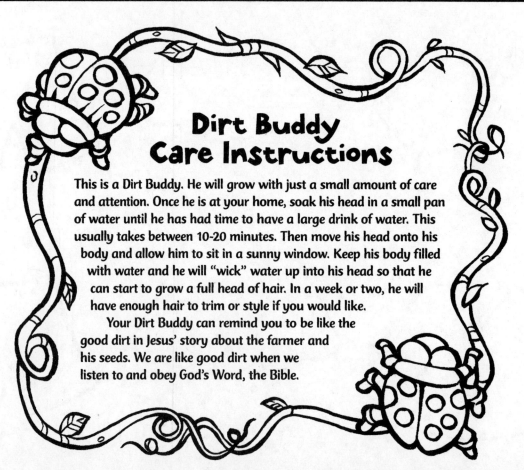

# Dirt Buddy
# Care Instructions

This is a Dirt Buddy. He will grow with just a small amount of care and attention. Once he is at your home, soak his head in a small pan of water until he has had time to have a large drink of water. This usually takes between 10-20 minutes. Then move his head onto his body and allow him to sit in a sunny window. Keep his body filled with water and he will "wick" water up into his head so that he can start to grow a full head of hair. In a week or two, he will have enough hair to trim or style if you would like.

Your Dirt Buddy can remind you to be like the good dirt in Jesus' story about the farmer and his seeds. We are like good dirt when we listen to and obey God's Word, the Bible.

# RAINFOREST STICKS (15-30 MINUTES)

## MATERIALS

- 9x12-inch (23x30.5-cm) construction paper
- rice
- spoons

**For each child—**
- 1 paper-towel tube
- 2 cupcake cups
- 2 toilet-paper tubes
- 3 colored rubber bands

## STANDARD SUPPLIES

- crayons
- craft glue or glue sticks

## INSTRUCT EACH CHILD IN THE FOLLOWING PROCEDURES:

- Select a sheet of construction paper. Color your paper with designs and shapes that remind you of God's amazing rainforest—blue for lakes, rivers or the sky, green for the color of trees, brown for the color of crocodiles or the dark soil that helps the forest grow. You can add spots or stripes to remind you of the animals that live under the rainforest canopy.
- Ask an adult to help you roll your decorated paper around the paper-towel tube, decorated side out (sketch a). Glue the edge and wrap one of the rubber bands around the tube. The rubber band both decorates the tube and helps hold the paper in place as the glue dries.
- Glue one of the cupcake cups to one end of your tube (sketch b). Wrap a rubber band around the cupcake cup to secure.
- Twist and crinkle the toilet-paper tubes and insert into rain stick. Use spoon to add 2 spoonfuls of rice to tube (sketch c).
- Glue the other cupcake cup to the other end of your tube. Wrap a rubber band around the cupcake cup to secure.

**Simplification Idea**
- In addition to drawing on papers, children decorate tubes with rainforest stickers (SonQuest Stickers available from Gospel Light).

**Enrichment Idea**
Arrange with music leader for children to use rain sticks during the Music Center and/or the Closing Program.

a.

b.

**Budget Tip:** Instead of paper towel tubes, roll 6x11-inch (15x28-cm) rectangles of card stock into a tube. Instead of toilet-paper tubes, use 4x6-inch (10x15-cm) index cards or card stock.

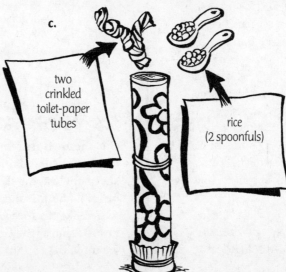

c.

two crinkled toilet-paper tubes

rice (2 spoonfuls)

## CONVERSATION

When we tilt our rain sticks, we hear a sound like rain. God wants us to hear and obey His Word, the Bible. In Psalm 119:11, our Bible says, "I have hidden your word in my heart." This means that we listen to and obey God's Word. When we do that, we Get It!

# SHEEP VISOR (15-30 MINUTES)

## MATERIALS

- Sheep Patterns (pp. 24-26)
- black permanent marker
- adhesive-backed craft foam (black and white)

**For each child—**

- 12x18-inch (30.5x45.5-cm) piece of white craft foam
- 2 20-mm wiggle eyes
- 20-30 cotton balls
- 5 or 6 spring-type clothespins
- curly shoelace

## STANDARD SUPPLIES

- white card stock
- scissors
- pencil
- white crayon or pencil
- craft glue

## PREPARATION

Photocopy Sheep Patterns onto white card stock and cut out. Use pencil to trace patterns (all but Nose) onto white craft foam. Cut out pattern pieces. Use white crayon or pencil to trace Nose Pattern onto black adhesive-backed craft foam and cut out.

Place Sheep Face Bottom Pattern on each craft-foam face bottom you cut out. Use a pencil to poke holes through the pattern into foam piece, transferring the mouth design to the craft foam (sketch a). Use black permanent marker to connect the pencil dots and draw the mouth (sketch b).

Use hole punch to punch a hole at each corner of the Sheep Face Bottom. From white adhesive-backed craft foam, cut a circle approximately 1-inch (2.5-cm) across. Cut two circles for each child. Punch a hole in a circle, align with one of the holes on the Sheep Face Bottom and adhere pieces together to form reinforcement for the hole. Continue, making reinforcements for both holes on all the visors (sketch c).

For each child, fold tabs on Sheep Face Top. Glue tabs to Sheep Face Bottom. Use clothespins to hold pieces together as glue sets (sketch d).

## INSTRUCT EACH CHILD IN THE FOLLOWING PROCEDURES:

- Place nose on top of mouth. Glue eyes to visor above nose (sketch e).
- Pull cotton balls slightly to make them fluffier. Glue cotton balls on four hearts to make sheep's wool (sketch f).
- Glue ears and hearts covered with cotton-balls to the top of your visor. Ask an adult to help you place clothespins to hold pieces in place as glue dries (sketch g).
- Ask an adult to help thread a curly shoelace through the holes in the visor (sketch h) and adjust it to fit your head.

**Simplification Idea**

Draw squiggly lines on the hearts instead of attaching cotton balls.

**Enrichment Idea**

Have children attach short lengths of white yarn to the ears and the visor brim above the face to make the lambs more wooly.

**Time-Saver Tips:** Instead of tracing and cutting Sheep Face Bottom pattern, use pre-made visors (available at craft stores). Use a 4-inch (10-cm) die to cut Sheep Wool pieces from craft foam.

**Budget Tips:** Make the visors out of poster board. Instead of using curly shoelaces, use 6-inch (15-cm) lengths of elastic. Staple elastic to visor and cover staples with a piece of adhesive-backed craft foam.

## CONVERSATION

**Our sheep visors remind us of the story Jesus told about a shepherd and his sheep. When one of the sheep got lost, the shepherd looked and looked until he found his lost sheep. God is like the shepherd and we are like His sheep. God doesn't want any of us to be lost. That's why God sent Jesus to Earth—so that we could Get Found!**

a.

b.

c.

d.

e.

f.

g.

h.

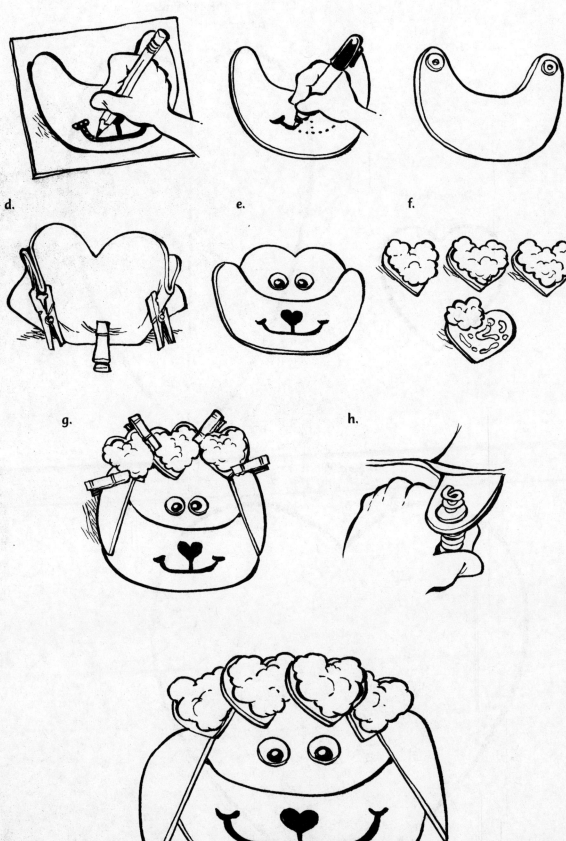

# SHEEP PATTERNS

**Sheep Ears**
cut on dotted line to separate ears

**Sheep Nose**

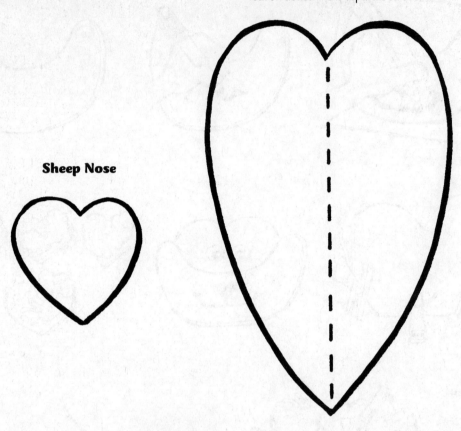

**Sheep Wool**
cut four

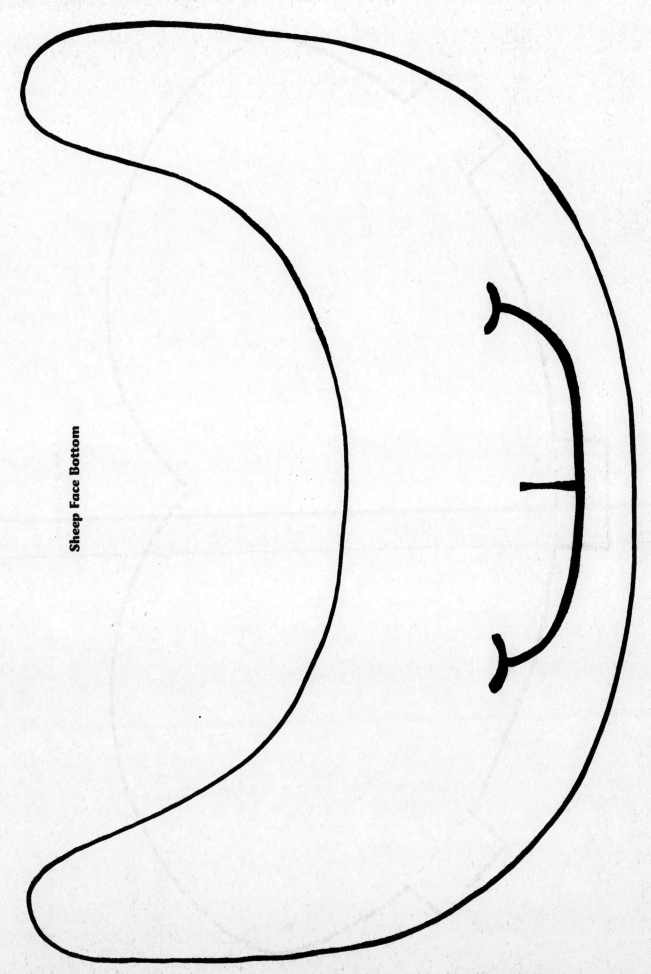

**Sheep Face Bottom**

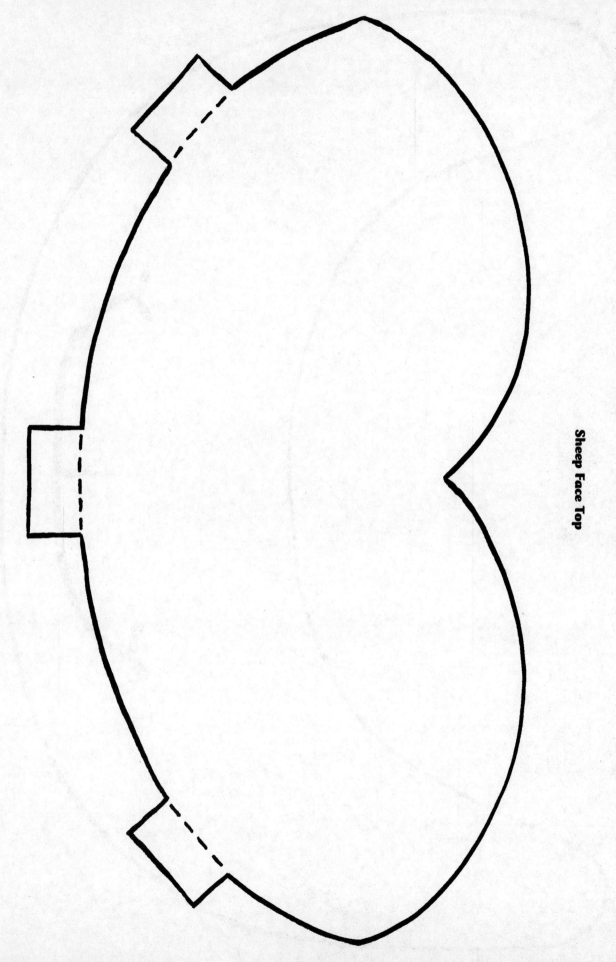

Sheep Face Top

# Good Samaritan Traveling Pouch **(15-20 MINUTES)**

## MATERIALS

- light-colored flannel-backed vinyl
- leather lacing
- rainforest stickers (SonQuest Stickers available from Gospel Light)

**For each child—**
- 4 wooden beads

## STANDARD SUPPLIES

- scissors
- hole punch

## PREPARATION

For each child, cut vinyl into a 6x16-inch (15x40.5-cm) rectangle (sketch a). Fold each vinyl piece in half so that the fold forms the bottom of the pouch. Punch six holes on either side of each bag, through both front and back of pouch (sketch b).

For each child, cut leather lacing into a 5-foot (1.5-m) length. Tie a knot at one end of each lacing length (sketch c).

> **Budget Tip:** Instead of using vinyl, use manila folders. Cut the flap off the top of each envelope and punch holes as described above. In addition to decorating pouches with stickers, children can use markers and/or rubber stamps and stamp pads.

## CONVERSATION

**In today's story, Jesus told how the Good Samaritan was kind to the man who had been hurt. As the Samaritan traveled, he carried things in a pouch like the one we made today. Just like the Good Samaritan, we can choose to be kind to others, too! When we are kind, we show God's love. God's love is so amazing, that when we Get God's Love, we want to give it to others!**

## INSTRUCT EACH CHILD IN THE FOLLOWING PROCEDURES:

- String two beads on a length of leather lacing (sketch d).
- Thread the lacing through a bottom hole on one side of your pouch. Continue stitching in and out of the holes up one side, and then down the other (sketch e).
- When you've finished stitching, thread two more beads onto your lacing. Ask an adult to tie a knot at the end of your lacing and to write your name on the pouch using a permanent marker. Decorate pouch with rainforest stickers.

**Enrichment Idea**
Provide alphabet stickers and help children place stickers to spell out their names.

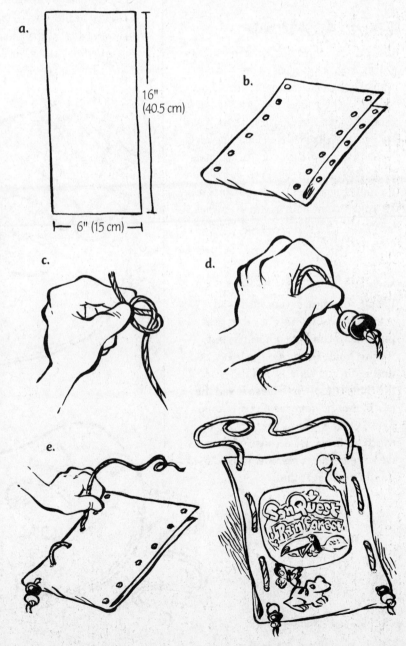

a.

16"
(40.5 cm)

6" (15 cm)

b.

c.

d.

e.

# RainFOREST MasK (15-30 MINUTES)

## MATERIALS

- Mask Pattern (p. 29)
- variety of craft foam
- variety of adhesive-backed craft foam
- yarn

## STANDARD SUPPLIES

- white card stock
- pencil
- scissors
- hole punch
- ruler

## PREPARATION

On card stock, photocopy Mask Pattern and cut out. For each child, use a pencil to trace Mask Pattern onto craft foam. Cut out the masks. Use hole punch to punch a hole on either side of the mask. Cut a variety of shapes from adhesive-backed craft foam, including two circles for each child. Punch a hole in each of the circles, align the holes over the holes on the masks and adhere to mask to form reinforcement for the holes (sketch a). Cut the yarn into 24-inch (61-cm) lengths, two for each child.

## CONVERSATION

People sometimes wear masks to pretend to be animals or other people. Masks can hide your face, but we can't hide from God. He loves us and is always with us. In John 3:16, the Bible says, "For God so loved the world that he gave his one and only Son." God sent Jesus to show how much He loves us! Because of Jesus, we can become a member of God's family and Get Found!

**Budget Tip:**
Use regular craft foam. Children glue shapes to masks.

## INSTRUCT EACH CHILD IN THE FOLLOWING PROCEDURES:

- Attach craft-foam shapes to decorate masks.
- Select two lengths of yarn. Ask a helper to thread the yarn through the holes on the sides of your mask, tying to secure.

### Simplification Ideas

- Instead of cutting shapes, use adhesive-backed craft foam shapes (available at craft stores).
- Children decorate masks with markers rather than craft-foam shapes.

### Enrichment Ideas

- Instead of tying yarn through holes on the sides of the mask, use a low-temperature glue gun to secure yarn to mask.
- Children cut their own shapes from craft foam.
- Children glue on other materials such as beads, small pieces of fabric, twine, yarn and/or feathers. Children can also attach additional lengths of yarn to which they string beads.

a.

# MASK PATTERN

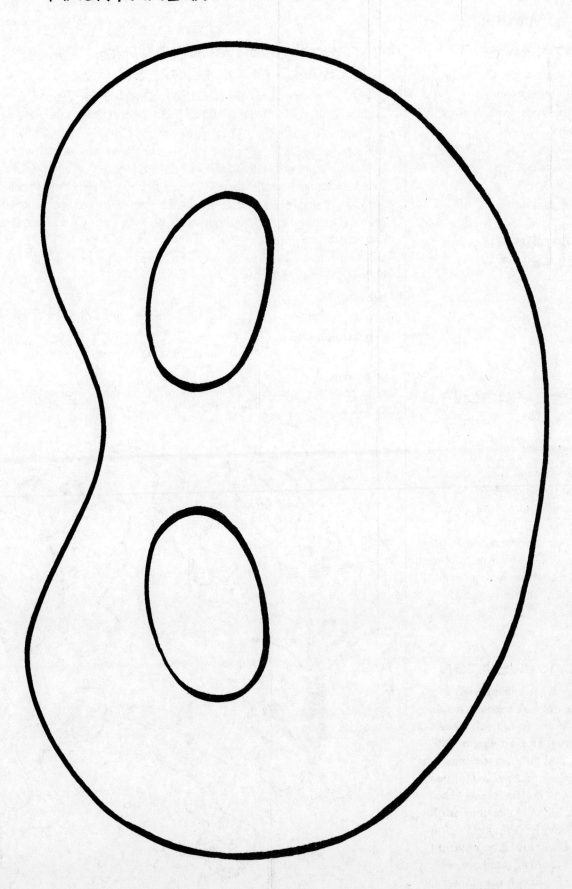

# Rainforest Animal Magnet

**(20-30 MINUTES)**

## MATERIALS

- Rainforest Animals Patterns (p. 31)
- variety of craft foam
- variety of adhesive-backed craft foam
- adhesive-backed magnetic strips
- 10-mm wiggle eyes
- chenille wires
- small pom-poms

## STANDARD SUPPLIES

- white card stock
- scissors
- pencils
- hole punches
- glue

## PREPARATION

On card stock, photocopy Rainforest Animals Patterns, making enough copies so that there is at least one pattern for each child, with some additional to provide plenty of choice for children. Cut out patterns. Cut craft foam into 5x8-inch (12.5x20.5-cm) pieces. Cut adhesive-backed craft foam into 2x2-inch (5x5-cm) pieces. For each child, cut adhesive-backed magnetic strips into 2-inch (5-cm) pieces.

## CONVERSATION

**Today we made magnets of some animals who are neighbors in the rainforest. We're learning about neighbors today, and how we can show God's love to them. In Matthew 22:37-39 our Bibles say, "Love the Lord. . . . Love your neighbor." EVERYONE is our neighbor! God's love is so amazing, when we Get God's Love, we want to share it with others.**

## INSTRUCT EACH CHILD IN THE FOLLOWING PROCEDURES:

- Choose a pattern and a large piece of craft foam for the body of your animal. Use a pencil to trace pattern onto craft foam and cut out (sketch a). Ask an adult to help you as needed.
- If you are making a snake or a gecko, glue wiggle eyes on your animal (sketch b).
- If you are making a butterfly, instead of gluing on wiggle eyes, wrap chenille wire around the body of your butterfly. Twist the chenille wires at the top and curl the ends to make antennae (sketch c). Glue pom-poms on the front to make the body of your butterfly (sketch d).
- Choose some small pieces of adhesive-backed craft foam to make dots to decorate your animal. Use a hole punch to punch out lots of dots, peel the paper off the backs of the dots and place them on your animal.
- Flip the animal upside-down, peel paper from back of magnetic strip and to place on the back of your animal (sketch f).

**Alternate Idea**
Instead of magnetic strips, provide jewelry pins. Children make pins instead of magnets.

**Simplification Idea**
Provide paint pens for the children to use in decorating their animal magnets.

**Enrichment Idea**
Provide additional materials for children to use to decorate their animals: glitter glue, jewels, beads, etc.

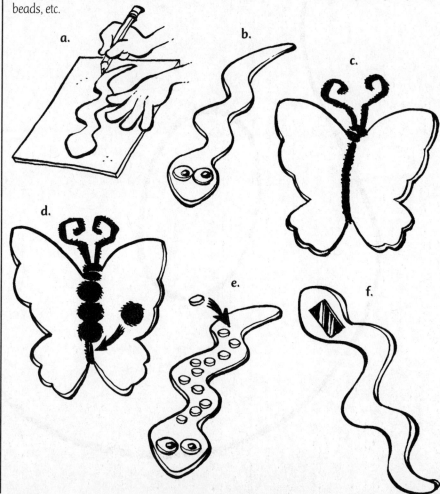

# RAINFOREST ANIMALS PATTERNS

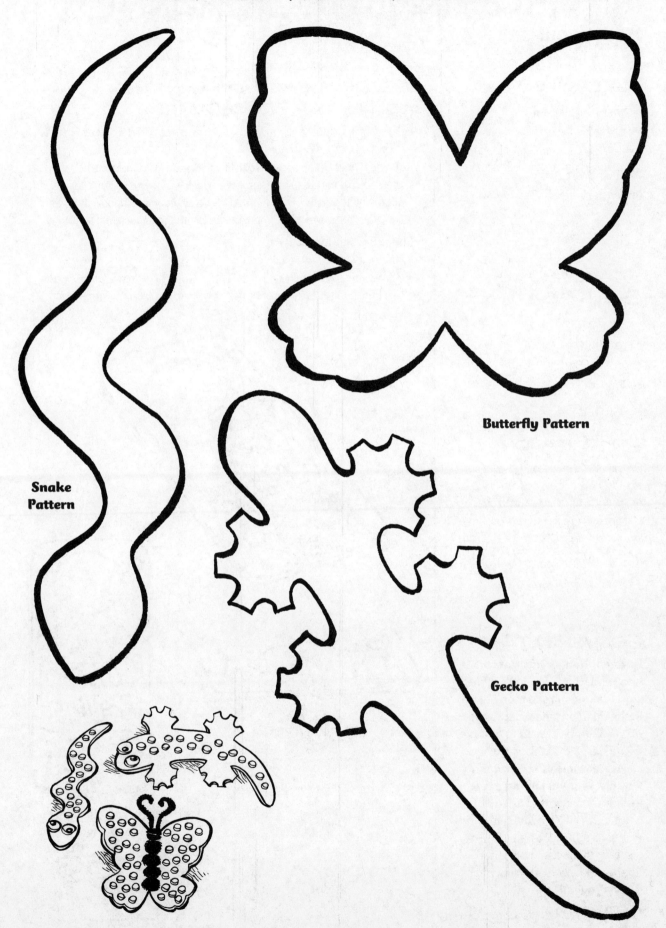

**Butterfly Pattern**

**Snake Pattern**

**Gecko Pattern**

# Get Praying! Door Hanger

## (15-20 MINUTES)

## MATERIALS

- Door Hanger Pattern (p. 33)
- craft foam
- star stickers or craft-foam star shapes
- yarn

**For each child—**
- adhesive label
- two jingle bells

## STANDARD SUPPLIES

- white card stock
- pencil
- scissors
- ruler
- hole punch

## PREPARATION

On card stock, photocopy and cut out Door Hanger Pattern. For each child, use pencil to trace pattern on a piece of craft foam and cut out. Print "Get Praying!" on adhesive labels. For each child, cut a 12-inch (30.5-cm) length of yarn.

## CONVERSATION

**Our door hanger has stars on it to remind us of today's Bible story. In our story, a man got up in the middle of the night to ask his neighbor for bread to feed his friend. Jesus told this story because He wants us to know that God gives us what we need. We just need to pray and ask God for what we need. God loves us and wants us to pray to Him. When we hear the bells on our door hanger jingle, we can remember to Get Praying!**

## INSTRUCT EACH CHILD IN THE FOLLOWING PROCEDURES:

- Place "Get Praying!" label on door hanger. Decorate with star stickers or craft-foam star shapes (sketch a).
- Thread a jingle bell on each end of a length of yarn. Ask a helper to help you tie a knot to secure the bells on the yarn. Then ask helper to find the center of the yarn length and thread the center through the hole in your door hanger, from front to back; then bring loop to the front, drop bells through the loop and tighten.

**Simplification Ideas**
- Pre-made foam door hangers are available at craft stores.
- Use a computer and printer to print "Get Praying!" on adhesive labels. Or use "Get Praying!" stickers from SonQuest Stickers (available from Gospel Light).

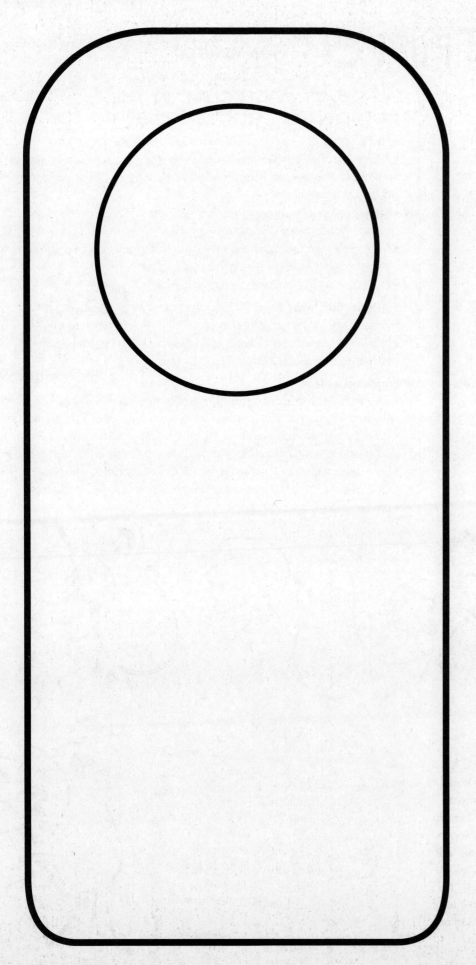

DOOR
HANGER
PATTERN

# PARROT PUPPET (15-30 MINUTES)

## MATERIALS
- variety of craft foam
- jumbo craft sticks

**Optional—**
- wiggle eyes

## STANDARD SUPPLIES
- scissors
- ruler
- markers
- craft glue

## PREPARATION
For each child, cut craft-foam sheets into one 9x12-inch (23x 30.5-cm) piece and one 6x9-inch (15x23-cm) piece, using a variety of colors. Cut additional shapes from craft foam.

## INSTRUCT EACH CHILD IN THE FOLLOWING PROCEDURES:
- Choose one larger piece of craft foam and another piece of a different color.
- Ask a helper to use a marker to trace around your two hands on the larger piece of craft foam. Take off a shoe and trace around your shoe on the smaller piece of foam (sketch a). Cut out traced shapes.
- Arrange and glue the shapes so that the shoe shape is the body, one hand is the tail, and the other hand is the wing (sketch b).
- Decorate the parrot with other shapes. You can use the shapes for a beak, feathers and eyes (sketch c). (Optional: Glue wiggle eyes to puppet.)
- Glue the jumbo craft stick on the back of the parrot.

### Simplification Ideas
- Helpers help children cut out the shapes.
- Instead of cutting additional shapes, use adhesive-backed craft foam shapes (available at craft stores).

### Enrichment Ideas
- Trace each child's hand and arm on a large piece of craft foam. Children cut out these shapes to become branches and decorate them with small pieces of craft foam to make leaves, buds, fruit, seeds and flowers. The branch can be attached at the base of the puppet, or held separately so that the children can use it as a prop in their own puppet plays.
- Use black craft foam for body, wings and tail. Make large beaks from yellow craft foam. Children make Toucan puppets and decorate beaks with colored foam shapes.
- Children attach feathers to puppets.

> **Budget Tip:** Use construction paper instead of craft foam.

a.

b.

c.

## CONVERSATION
**Parrots are colorful, fun birds. They are different from most birds because they can be trained to talk. God loves us and wants us to talk to Him. When we talk to God, it's called prayer. In Philippians 4:6 our Bible says, "By prayer . . . present your requests to God." We can talk to God at any time about anything!**

> **Note:** Trace very roughly around children's hand. The shapes should be very rounded and more of a suggestion of fingers, rather than an exact tracing of the child's hand. The rounder the shapes, the more easily children can cut around them. For younger children, you may want to simply trace around the child's closed hand.

# Rainforest Talent Box

**(15-20 MINUTES)**

## MATERIALS

- rubber stamps
- washable ink pads
- rainforest stickers (SonQuest Stickers available from Gospel Light)

**For each child—**

- small paper mache or wooden box

## INSTRUCT EACH CHILD IN THE FOLLOWING PROCEDURES:

- Place stamps on ink pads to ink the stamps. Then press stamps on box to decorate.
- Also decorate box with rainforest stickers.

### Enrichment Ideas

- Instead of rainforest stickers, provide a variety of stickers representing different talents (sports, horses, books, art supplies, dance, etc.). Children decorate boxes with stickers representing talents or abilities they have.

## CONVERSATION

**In our Bible story, we heard about a man who trusted his servants with some of his money. We can use these Talent Boxes to save money we earn from chores or other work we do. What are some ways we can spend the money to serve others?** (Give to missions projects. Donate to an animal shelter.) **We show love for God when we serve others.**

**Note:** When placing a sticker on the side of the box, if sticker overlaps the lid, cut the sticker so that half is on the lid and half is on the side of the box.

# BUTTERFLY WRISTBANDS (20-30 MINUTES)

## MATERIALS

- Butterfly Pattern from Rainforest Animals Patterns (p. 31)
- 8½x11-inch (21.5x28-cm) transparency sheets (available at office-supply stores)
- variety of tissue paper, including several shades of blue
- chenille wires
- yarn

**For every 2 children—**
- toilet paper tube
- bowl

## STANDARD SUPPLIES

- newspaper
- scissors
- ruler
- white glue
- water
- foam paintbrushes
- hole punch

**Note:** Be sure to use transparency sheets specially designed to be used in a photocopier or printer.

## PREPARATION

Cover tables with newspaper. Enlarge Butterfly Pattern to be approximately 8 inches (20.5 cm) across. Photocopy or print enlarged butterfly onto transparency sheets, making one butterfly for each child. Cut out butterflies. Cut tissue paper into squares approximately 1-inch (2.5-cm) in size. To make wristbands, slit toilet paper tubes vertically, and then cut in half (sketch a), making one wristband for each child. Mix equal parts water and glue in bowls, preparing one bowl for every two children.

For each child, cut yarn into an 8-inch (20.5-cm) length. Use hole punch to make a hole in either side of the wristbands you cut from the toilet paper tube. Thread yarn through each hole and tie in a bow to secure (sketch b).

## INSTRUCT EACH CHILD IN THE FOLLOWING PROCEDURES:

- Use foam paintbrushes to brush glue and water mixture onto butterfly. Place squares of tissue paper on butterfly's wings (sketch c). If any tissue-paper overlaps the edges of the wing, ask a helper to cut tissue paper.
- Place butterfly on wristband. Choose a chenille wire and ask an adult to help you wrap the chenille wire around the butterfly and wristband, twisting wires together at the top (sketch d). Use your finger to curl the ends of the chenille wire to make antennae.
- Ask an adult to help you tie wristband onto your wrist.

### Alternate Ideas
- Instead of transparencies, use construction paper to make wings.
- Children wrap tissue-paper squares around the eraser end of a pencil, dab with glue and place on wings, creating a "fluffy" butterfly!

### Budget Tip
Make your own paintbrushes. Cut sponges into 2-inch (5-cm) pieces. Clip a spring-type clothespin to make a handle (sketch e).

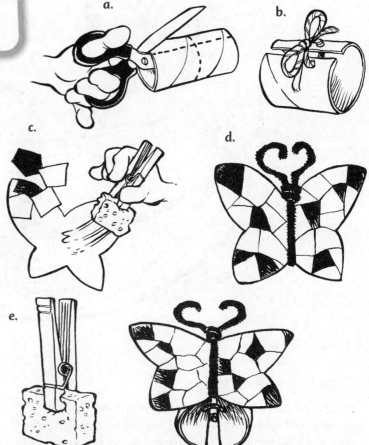

## CONVERSATION

**Butterflies are going all the time! They flutter up and down all through the rainforest. As they go, they help plants grow. God wants us to Get Going and use the abilities He's given us. In Colossians 3:23, our Bible says, "Whatever you do, work . . . for the Lord." When we are working for the Lord, it means we are doing our best work. When we use our abilities to serve others, we are working for God! We're showing that we love God.**

# SECTION TWO/GRADES 1-3
# CRAFTS FOR YOUNGER ELEMENTARY

Children in the first few years of school delight in completing craft projects. They have a handle on most of the basic skills needed, they are eager to participate, and their taste in art has usually not yet surpassed their ability to produce. In other words, they generally like what they make.

Because reading ability is not a factor in most craft projects, crafts can be a great leveler among children. Some children who are not top achievers in other areas excel here.

You may find additional projects suitable for younger elementary children in the first section of this book, "Crafts for Young Children."

# seed Bracelets (5-10 MINUTES)

## MATERIALS
- ⅜-inch (0.9-cm) diameter clear plastic tubing
- saw
- ¼-inch (0.6 cm) dowels
- variety of brightly colored duct tape
- birdseed and/or seed beads

**For every 3 or 4 children—**
- 2 bowls for birdseed and/or seed beads

## STANDARD SUPPLIES
- scissors
- craft glue

## PREPARATION
Use scissors to cut plastic tubing into 9-inch (23-cm) lengths, at least one for each child. Use saw to cut dowel into 1-inch (2.5-cm) pieces. Place birdseed and seed beads in bowls.

## INSTRUCT EACH CHILD IN THE FOLLOWING PROCEDURES:
- Measure plastic tubing to wrist. Add approximately 1 inch (2.5 cm) so that finished bracelet will fit over hand and cut.
- Cover one end of the dowel with glue and insert into one end of the tubing (sketch a).
- Use the open end of the tube to scoop birdseed or seed beads into the tubing (sketch b).
- Glue remaining dowel section and insert into the open end of the tube.
- Cover the glued section of the tube with duct tape (sketch c).

### Enrichment Idea
As time allows, children make additional bracelets to keep or give to friends, or children make necklaces by cutting 30-inch (76-cm) lengths of tubing.

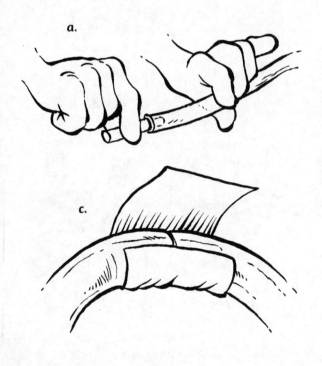

## CONVERSATION
Today's Bible story is a story Jesus told. The story is about a farmer and the seed he threw on different types of soil. People are like the types of soil in Jesus' story. God is like the farmer, and the seed is like His Word, the Bible. The seeds in our bracelets can remind us of God's Word and that He wants us to listen to and put into action the good things He tells us to do in the Bible.

Who can tell me the Daily Challenge we're talking about today? Pause for children to respond, "Get It." When we say we've Got It, we mean that we heard, understand and will do what the Bible tells us to do. So do you Get It? Encourage children to respond, "Got it!" Good!

# POM-POM SHEEP (20-30 MINUTES)

## MATERIALS

- Pom-Pom Sheep Pattern
- lightweight cardboard
- black chenille wires
- black narrow ribbon
- white yarn
- black felt

**For each child—**
- rubber band
- 2 10-mm wiggle eyes
- 7-mm red pom-pom
- ½-inch (1.3-cm) gold bell

## STANDARD SUPPLIES

- white card stock
- scissors
- glue
- white crayons or colored pencils

## PREPARATION

Photocopy Pom-Pom Sheep Pattern onto card stock, making one for each child. Cut to separate the patterns, but children will cut out the patterns themselves. Cut cardboard into 4x7-inch (10x18-cm) rectangles, one for each child. Cut ribbon into 10-inch (25.5-cm) lengths, one for each child. Cut chenille wires in half, making one 6-inch (15-cm) length for each child.

## CONVERSATION

**Our sheep can remind us of today's Bible story about a shepherd who lost one of his sheep. Jesus said that God is like the shepherd and we are like the sheep.**

**Who can tell me the Daily Challenge we're talking about today?** ("Get Found!") **Without Jesus, we're like lost sheep. But once we believe in Jesus as our Savior and become members of God's family, we can say that we've been found!**

## INSTRUCT EACH CHILD IN THE FOLLOWING PROCEDURES:

- Wrap yarn around the cardboard rectangle 80 times, counting as you wrap (sketch a). Wrap yarn loosely so it will easily be removed from the cardboard.
- When finished, slide the yarn off the cardboard onto your fingers, gathering all the loops together. Wrap the rubber band around the loops, center the rubber band, creating a shape like the numeral eight (sketch b).
- Cut the chenille pipe cleaner in half. Thread the two pieces through the rubber band and twist them a couple times so they stay in place. These will be the legs (sketch c).
- Cut the yarn loops and fluff them out to make the pom-pom (sketch d).
- Cut out the Pom-Pom Sheep Pattern from the card stock. Use white crayon or colored pencil to trace the pattern onto black felt and then cut it out. Glue felt face to the pom-pom sheep. Glue eyes and nose onto the face (sketch e).
- Use strands of yarn to tie the bell onto the sheep, below the face, use strands of yarn to secure the bell. Tie the ribbon to the center of the yarn pom-pom, creating a loop for hanging (sketch f).

### Simplification Idea

Before class, trace and cut out the sheep faces for the children.

a.

b.

c.

d.

e.

f.

**Pom-Pom Sheep Pattern**

# Rainforest Tic-Tac-Toe (30-40 MINUTES)

## MATERIALS

- Tic-Tac-Toe Patterns (pp. 41-42)
- variety of craft foam
- green felt
- resealable plastic bag
- permanent markers or paint pens

**For each child—**

- 8x10-inch (20.5x25.5-cm) clear acrylic box frame
- 5 sheets of craft foam: yellow, green, red, tan and white
- 12 20-mm wiggle eyes
- 12 12-mm wiggle eyes

## STANDARD SUPPLIES

- rulers
- scissors
- white card stock
- glue
- pencils

## PREPARATION

Cut green felt into 8x10-inch (20.5x25.5-cm) pieces. On card stock, photocopy Tic-Tac-Toe Patterns and cut out. Make a set of pattern pieces for every two or three children to use and share.

## INSTRUCT EACH CHILD IN THE FOLLOWING PROCEDURES:

- Cut yellow craft foam into 2¼x2½-inch (5.6x6.5-cm) pieces. Glue foam rectangles to the felt in a grid pattern, three across and three down (sketch a). Turn picture frame upside down and place felt inside.
- Trace the tall grass pattern onto green craft foam and cut out. Trace the other grass pattern onto green craft foam twice and cut out. Trace large and small flowers onto craft foam. Cut out and glue to grass (sketch b).
- Glue tall grass piece inside one of the long sides of the picture frame. Glue the other pieces of grass inside each of the short sides of the picture frame (sketch c).
- Trace six frog faces onto red craft foam and cut out. For each frog's face, use permanent markers or paint pens to draw a smile and glue on two large wiggle eyes (sketch d). (Optional: Cut smiles from scraps of craft foam and glue onto face.)
- Trace six monkey faces onto tan craft foam. Trace six manes on white craft foam. Cut out and glue together, manes on top of faces. Glue two smaller wiggle eyes onto each monkey's face. Using permanent markers or paint pens, draw small lines to represent the monkey's nose (sketch e).
- Place game pieces in resealable plastic bag.

### Simplification Ideas

- Instead of cutting and gluing flowers and leaves, use adhesive-backed craft-foam flowers and leaves (available at craft stores). Use adhesive-backed craft foam for the rectangles on the game board.
- Instead of using acrylic frames, glue craft-foam grass to edges of 8x10-inch (20.5x25.5-cm) pieces of green felt. Roll up board when not in use.

a.

b.

c.

d.

e.

# TIC-TAC-TOE PATTERNS

**small flower**

**monkey mane**

**large flower**

**monkey face**

**frog face**

## CONVERSATION

The frogs in our game look like Strawberry Dart Frogs, our animal for the day. What is today's Daily Challenge? (Get It!) Strawberry Dart Frogs "Get It" when it comes to living in the rainforest! They have suction cups on toes so they can climb trees and leaves. And their bright color helps their predators "Get It" that they are poisonous.

In Psalm 119:11, our Bible says, "I have hidden your word in my heart that I might not sin against you." "Sin" is a word used to describe the wrong things we do. When we read God's Word and obey it, God helps us live in the very best way. When we hide God's Word in our heart and show it by the way we live, then we show that we "Get It." Get it? *Encourage children to respond, "Got it!"* **Good!**

# Tic-Tac-Toe Patterns

**grass**

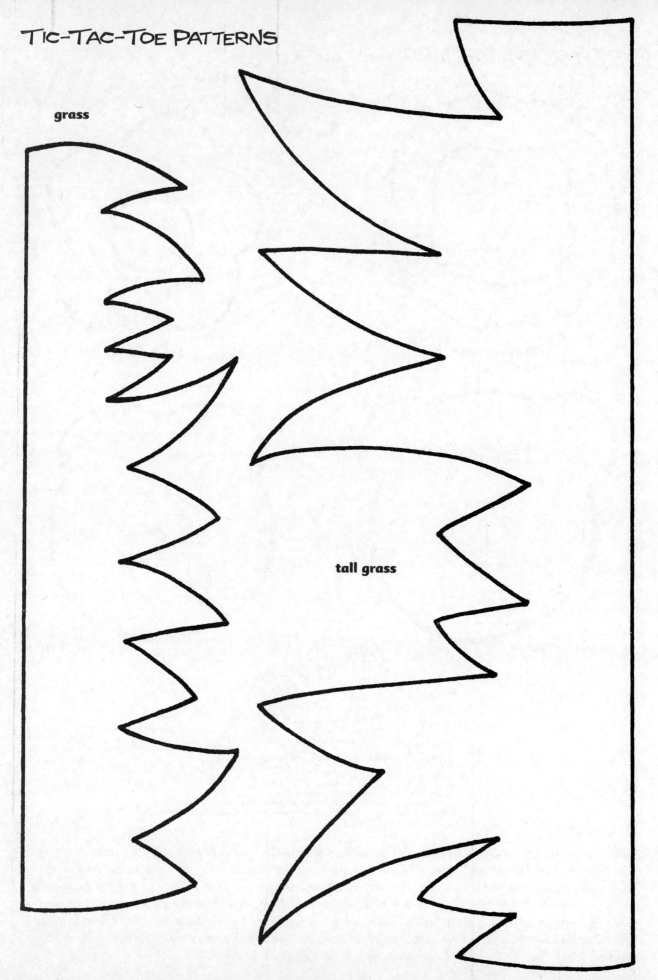

**tall grass**

**Younger Elementary · Grades 1-3**

# MaRaCas (15-20 MINUTES)

## MATERIALS

- variety of adhesive-backed craft-foam sheets and shapes
- glue remover (isopropyl alcohol, charcoal lighter fluid, commercial products, cooking oil, etc.)
- variety of acrylic paints
- ribbon
- plastic pony beads
- brightly colored duct tape
- variety of non-adhesive craft-foam shapes
- glitter

**For each child—**
- plastic bottle (any shape, 1-liter or smaller)
- 12-inch (30.5-cm) dowels

**Optional—**
- small jingle bells

## STANDARD SUPPLIES

- paintbrushes
- scissors

## PREPARATION

Cut ¾x9-inch (1.9x23-cm) strips of adhesive-backed craft foam, preparing one for each child. Clean and remove labels from bottles, using glue remover to remove excess glue. Wash bottles again. Paint dowels in a variety of colors.

## CONVERSATION

**We can use our maracas to sing SonQuest songs or other songs about God. Many songs, like "I Have Hidden Your Word" and "All My Heart" are like prayers, because we are talking to God when we sing the songs. God wants us to pray to Him. In Philippians 4:6-7, God's Word says, "Do not be anxious about anything, but in everything, by prayer and petition, with thanksgiving, present your requests to God. And the peace of God . . . will guard your hearts and your minds in Christ Jesus."**

    **What is the Daily Challenge for today?** Pause for children to respond, "Get Praying." **When times are difficult, it's good to remember that God always listens to our prayers, and we can always have His peace by trusting in Him. So how about it? Are you ready to Get Praying?** Encourage children to respond, "Got Praying!" **Good!**

## INSTRUCT EACH CHILD IN THE FOLLOWING PROCEDURES:

- Choose a dowel and tie ribbon and beads to it, using thin strips of duct tape to secure ribbons and/or for additional decoration (sketch a).
- Push the dowel into the bottle, so that the ribbons and beads are inside the bottle. Push the dowel to the bottom of the bottle so the dowel can not move. Use a pencil to make a mark on the dowel at the neck of the bottle (sketch b).
- Pull the dowel out of the bottle. Wrap the foam strip around the dowel to cushion and support the dowel at the neck of the bottle (sketch c).
- Inside the bottle, add some non-adhesive craft-foam shapes, beads and/or glitter (sketch d). (Optional: Add small jingle bells.)
- Push the dowel back into the bottle. Secure by winding duct tape around the neck of the bottle and the dowel (sketch e).
- Decorate the outside of the bottle by adding adhesive-backed craft-foam shapes and/or ribbon and beads.

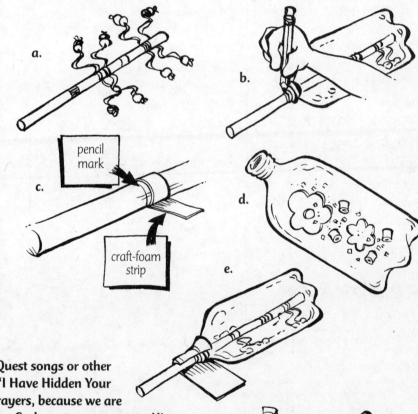

a.

b.

c.

pencil mark

craft-foam strip

d.

e.

# DRAGONFLY (30 MINUTES)

## MATERIALS

- Wing Pattern (p. 45)
- plastic drinking straws
- variety of colored paper
- paint for Styrofoam
- paintbrush
- Styrofoam block
- iridescent glitter
- bowls
- spoons
- yarn
- low-temperature glue gun
- ¼-inch (0.6-cm) ribbon

### For each child—

- 4-inch (10-cm) Styrofoam ball
- craft needle
- 5 9-oz. colored paper cups
- 2 transparency sheets
- 2-inch (5-cm) pom-pom
- 2 20-mm wiggle eyes
- chenille wire

## STANDARD SUPPLIES

- white card stock
- scissors
- rulers
- pencils
- glue
- transparent tape

## PREPARATION

For each child, photocopy the Wing Pattern onto card stock. Cut straws into 3-inch (7.5-cm) lengths, making four for each child. Pour glitter into several bowls. Place spoons in bowls.

Place Styrofoam ball on a pencil to use pencil as a handle to paint Styrofoam ball. Paint until covered, usually two coats. Place other end of pencil in Styrofoam block to dry (sketch a). (**Important Note:** Use only paints specifically designed to work on Styrofoam. Other paints, especially spray paints, can melt the Styrofoam.)

## INSTRUCT EACH CHILD IN THE FOLLOWING PROCEDURES:

- Place the Wing Pattern under one of the transparency sheets. Trace the Wing Pattern with glue and then use spoon to sprinkle glitter over the glue (sketch b). Shake extra glitter back into the bowl.
- Cut a 30-inch (76-cm) piece of yarn and thread it through a craft needle. Tie a knot at the end. Begin assembling your dragonfly by pushing the needle through the bottom of one of the cups you covered. Next, string a piece of straw and then another cup (sketch d). Continue alternating cups and pieces of straw until all five cups have been strung. Tie a knot at the end of your yarn; tape to the bottom of the top cup securely.
- When glue is dry, cut out the wings, leaving ¼-inch (0.6-cm) edge around the glitter lines (sketch d).
- Glue wiggle eyes on to painted Styrofoam ball. Glue pom-pom to ball to make a nose. Cut chenille wire in half and push each piece into Styrofoam ball to make antennae. Curl the chenille-wire ends (sketch e).
- Ask an adult to use the low-temperature glue gun to attach the wings and head onto your dragonfly.
- Cut a 15-inch (38-cm) length of ribbon and tie around the dragonfly's neck to make a loop for hanging.

### Simplification Idea
Instead of sprinkling glitter on glue, use glitter glue.

### Enrichment Idea
Use glitter glue or paint pens to decorate cups.

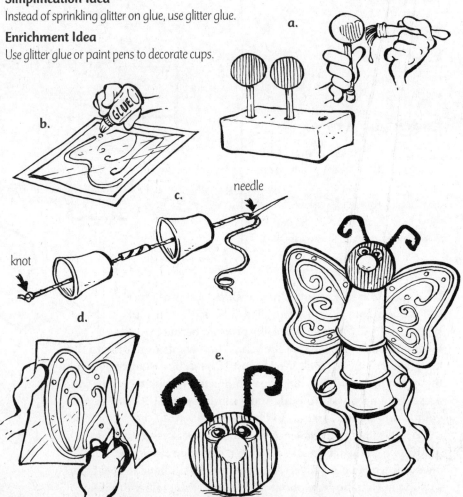

a.

b.

c.

needle

knot

d.

e.

## CONVERSATION

Have you ever heard of "oding"? Oding is the hobby of trying to find dragonflies! What is the Daily Challenge for today? *Pause for children to respond,* "Get Found!" When we talk about "Get(ting) Found," we're talking about becoming a member of God's family. God sent Jesus to Earth because He loves us! When Jesus died and rose again, He made it possible for us to live with Him forever!

In John 3:16 the Bible says, "For God so loved the world that he gave his one and only Son, that whoever believes in him shall not perish but have eternal life." God wants each of us to Get Found and become a member of His family. So how about it? Did anyone here Get Found? *Willing children respond,* "Got found!" Good!

# Palm Leaf Mouse Pad

**(15-20 MINUTES)**

## MATERIALS

- Palm Leaf Pattern (p. 47)
- variety of adhesive-backed craft foam
- permanent markers, gel pens and/or paint pens

**For each child—**
- sheet of green craft foam

## STANDARD SUPPLIES

- white card stock
- scissors

## PREPARATION

On card stock, photocopy Palm Leaf Pattern, making one for each child.

## CONVERSATION

Jesus told the parable of the Good Samaritan to explain that just like the Samaritan did, we can obey God by showing love and giving help to all people—even if it isn't easy or convenient.

Who can tell me the Daily Challenge we're talking about today? Pause for children to respond, "Get God's Love!" God's love is so AMAZING that once we get it, we want to share it with others! Jesus wants us to think not only about ourselves, but also to put other people's needs ahead of what we want. He wants us to help others, even when it means doing something we don't like or helping someone who isn't popular with our friends. So are you ready to help others and Get God's Love? Encourage children to respond, "Got God's Love!" Good!

## INSTRUCT EACH CHILD IN THE FOLLOWING PROCEDURES:

- Cut out pattern from card stock. Use a marker or gel pen to trace pattern onto craft foam (sketch a). Cut out leaf.
- Use markers and/or gel pens to draw leaf details and print "Get God's Love!" on your leaf.
- Use adhesive-backed craft foam to cut out flowers and bugs to decorate your palm leaf. Be sure to place flowers and bugs around the edges, so your computer mouse can move freely around the center of the leaf.

**Simplification Ideas**

- Use scraps of regular craft foam to make flowers and bugs. Children glue shapes to Palm Leaf Mouse Pad.
- Use craft-foam die-cuts shaped like flowers and bugs (available at craft stores).

PALM LEAF PATTERN

Get God's Love!

# GeT PRAYiNG! CHALKBOARD (20-30 MINUTES)

## MATERIALS

- Get Praying! Daily Challenge color image (available on CD-ROM)
- plastic knife
- chalkboard paint (available at craft stores)
- waxed paper
- play-dough rollers or brayers (do not use utensils used in food preparation)
- ultra thick embossing powder
- baking sheets

**For every two children—**
- 2-oz. package of polymer clay in green, gold and white

**For each child—**
- resealable plastic bag
- toothpick
- unfinished wood frame (available at craft stores)

## STANDARD SUPPLIES

- white paper
- ballpoint pens
- white glue

## PREPARATION

Use your computer to size the color image of the Get Praying! Daily Challenge. Enlarge or shrink the image to fit in the center top of the wooden frames you chose. For each child, print the image on white paper.

Use plastic knife to cut each package of clay in half, creating 1-oz. pieces of green, gold and white clay for each child. Put the three pieces of clay in a resealable plastic bag.

Follow the directions on your chalkboard paint canister and use paintbrushes to paint the cardboard inserts that came with your frames (sketch a). Set aside any glass that may have come with the frames.

## INSTRUCT EACH CHILD IN THE FOLLOWING PROCEDURES:

- Cut out the Get Praying paper, leaving some of the white paper around the edges of the image (sketch b).

- Place a sheet of waxed paper on the table where you will be working. Condition the clay by taking the white piece and kneading, folding and rolling it for a couple of minutes. Do the same thing with the green and gold clay, but work these two colors together at the same time, blending the colors together. You'll know the clay is properly conditioned when you can roll it into a log, fold it and the clay doesn't break (sketch c).

- Use play-dough rollers or brayers to flatten white clay into a slab slightly larger than Get Praying! paper. Place a thin layer of white glue on the back of the Get Praying! Paper and place on the slab of clay. Use a toothpick to trace around the paper. Do not trace directly along the edge of the paper, but allow for a thin clay margin around the edges (sketch d). Put the remaining white clay back in the plastic bag and seal it.

- Roll about half the green/gold clay into a long thin log (sketch e). Place the log along all the edges of the Get Praying clay piece. Press lightly to adhere the log to the white clay around the edges of the paper (sketch f).

- Use ballpoint pen to print your name on the back of your picture frame. Place some glue at the center top of your wooden frame (sketch g). Place Get Praying! clay piece on the glue (sketch h).

- Use play-dough rollers or brayers to flatten green/gold clay into a thin slab. Use toothpick to cut out leaf shapes (sketch i). Use end of toothpick to draw veins on the leaves.

- Place a thin line of glue on the back of each leaf and place on frame to decorate (sketch j). Place as many leaves as you want on your frame.

- Roll remaining green/gold clay into a long thin log. Make swirly and curly vines with the logs to fill in any empty space on the frame (sketch k). Place thin lines of glue under the vines as you go.

- Sprinkle ultra thick embossing powder over the Get Praying paper (sketch l). Use a toothpick to spread the powder all over the paper, but do not worry if it isn't completely even. It will even out as it melts in the oven.

- Line baking sheets with waxed paper. Place frame on a baking sheet. After class, leader places baking sheets in oven and bakes according to polymer clay manufacturer's instructions. (Usually 265°F or 275°F for 15 to 20 minutes.) You can bake in either a regular oven or toaster oven. Allow frames to cool completely before removing from the baking sheet.

**Simplification Idea**
Instead of making the Get Praying! piece at the top of the frame, cover the entire frame with clay leaves and vines. Children may also make rainforest animals or bugs from other colors of clay to decorate their frames.

## CONVERSATION

On our chalkboards, we can write things we want to pray about. In Jesus' story about knocking on a neighbor's door Jesus teaches us to pray when we have a problem or when we want something.

Who can tell me the Daily Challenge we're talking about today? Pause for children to respond, "Get Praying!" When we need something or are feeling sad, angry or scared, the best thing we can do is talk to God. Because we can pray to God about anything, at any time, we can always have peace. Having peace means we know that whatever happens, God is with us, that God is good and He provides what we need. So are you ready to Get Praying? Encourage children to respond, "Got Praying!" Good!

# CAPUCHIN SOCK MONKEY (30 MINUTES)

## MATERIALS

- Capuchin Patterns (pp. 51-52)
- fiberfill
- black yarn
- black felt
- tan felt
- white felt
- ¼-inch pom-poms

**For each child—**
- adult-sized black knee high or sock
- 2 12-mm wiggle eyes
- 5 safety pins

## STANDARD SUPPLIES

- white card stock
- white and dark crayons or colored pencils
- craft glue
- scissors

## PREPARATION

For each child, photocopy Capuchin Patterns onto card stock.

## INSTRUCT EACH CHILD IN THE FOLLOWING PROCEDURES:

- Stuff the sock until half of the sock is filled. Using the yarn, wrap the yarn around the sock at the top of the stuffing to make a neck. Tie a knot to secure (sketch a), place a drop of glue on the knot and trim yarn ends close to the knot.
- Stuff half of the remaining sock. Tie yarn in a tight knot at the top of the stuffing (sketch b). Fold the remaining end of the sock over to form head (sketch c).
- Cut out Capuchin Patterns. Use a white crayon or colored pencil to trace two arms, two legs and a tail onto the black felt (sketch d). Cut out.
- Use a dark crayon or colored pencil to trace the face, two hands, and two feet onto the tan felt. Cut out.
- Use a dark crayon or colored pencil to trace the mane and tummy onto the white felt. Cut out.
- Glue the white mane onto the tan face. Glue the wiggle eyes onto face. Glue the pom-pom under eyes to make a nose (sketch e). Glue face onto the head of the sock monkey.
- Glue the hands and feet onto the arms and legs. Using safety pins, secure the arms, legs and tail onto the monkey.

**Simplification Idea**
Precut felt pieces.

**Enrichment Ideas**
- Try red, purple, green or blue safety pins. These can be purchased at craft stores.
- Use white faux fur for the monkey mane and tummy.
- Add a bow tie made from a bright color of felt or a ribbon.
- Attach Velcro® dots to hands and feet so that hands and/or feet can be clasped.

# CAPUCHIN PATTERNS

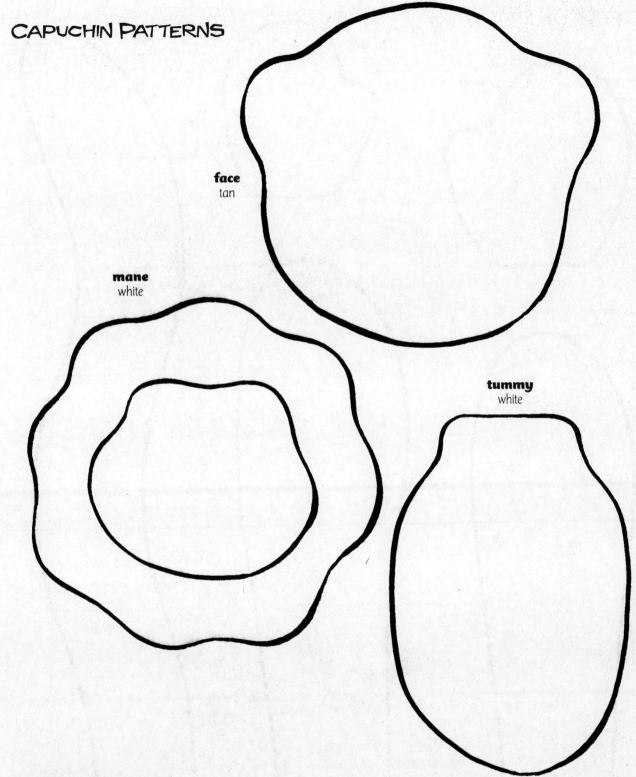

**face**
tan

**mane**
white

**tummy**
white

# CONVERSATION

Our animal today is the Capuchin Monkey. Not only are capuchin monkeys very friendly, but they are often trained as special helpers for people with physical needs. Helping others isn't always easy. God wants us to be willing to show His love to others. Matthew 22:37-39 is often referred to as the greatest commandment because when someone asked Jesus which was the greatest commandment, He answered by saying these words: "Love the Lord your God with all your heart and with all your soul and with all your mind. . . . Love your neighbor as yourself."

**What is the Daily Challenge for today?** Pause for children to respond, "Get God's Love!" **So how about it? Are you ready to Get God's Love?** Encourage children to respond, "Got God's Love!" **Good!**

# CAPUCHIN PATTERNS

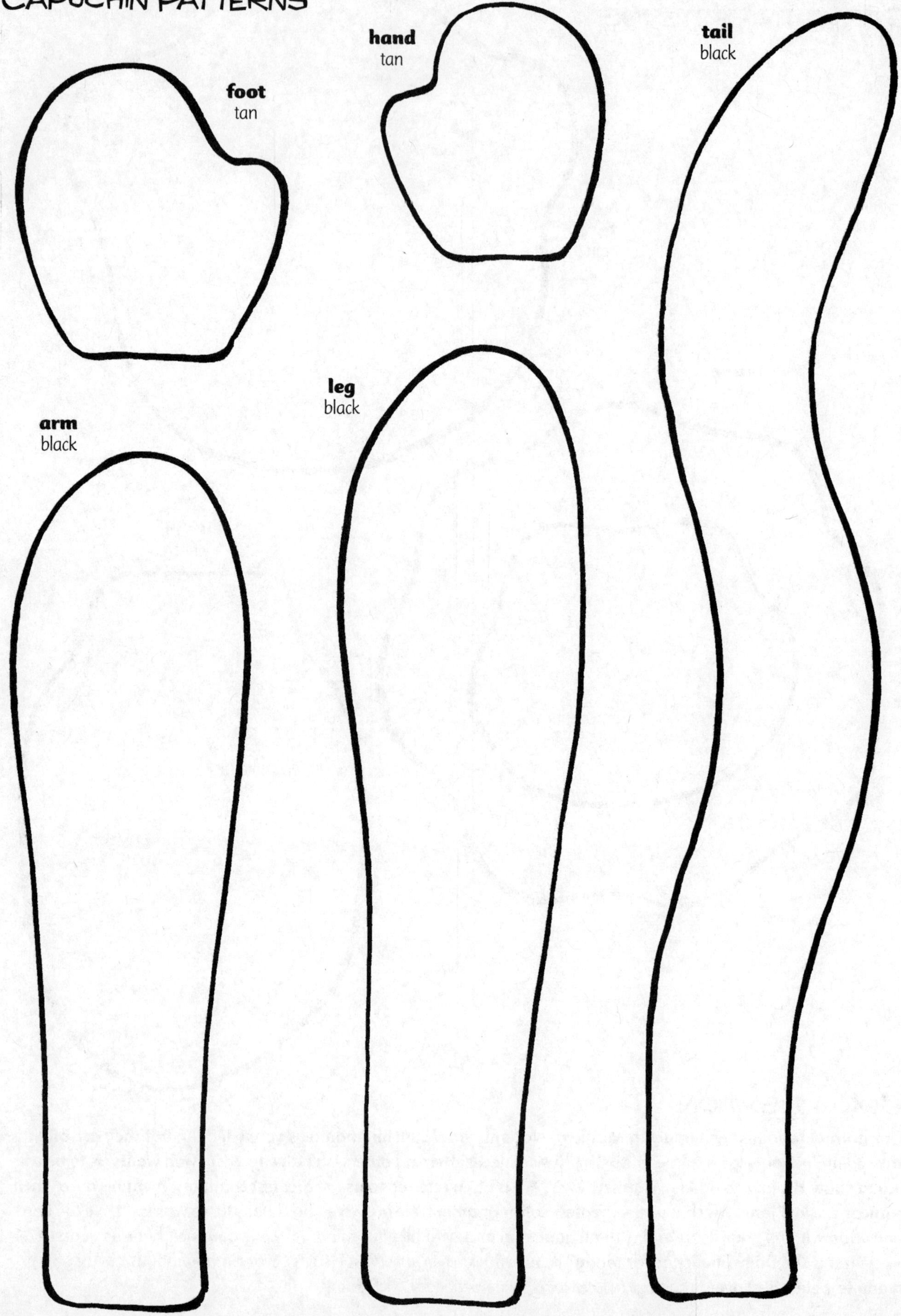

**hand**
tan

**foot**
tan

**tail**
black

**arm**
black

**leg**
black

# TARGET GAME (20-30 MINUTES)

## MATERIALS

- Target Words (p. 54)
- red, green, blue, yellow felt
- ¼-inch (0.6-cm) diameter dowels
- ¾-inch (1.9-cm) adhesive-backed Velcro®
- ¼-inch (0.6-cm) ribbon
- large craft needles

**For each child—**
- resealable plastic bag
- 6 ping pong balls

**Optional—**
- clear packing tape

## STANDARD SUPPLIES

- white card stock
- scissors
- glue

## PREPARATION

Photocopy Target Words onto card stock, one for every four children. Cut each word strip apart, making one strip for each child. Cut blue, green and yellow felt into 9-inch (23-cm) squares. Cut red felt into an 18x20-inch (45.5x51-cm) rectangle. Separate Velcro, reserving the hook side. Cut hook side into 42-inch (106-cm) lengths, one for every two children. Cut each length of the hook side vertically, to make strips ⅜-inch (0.9-cm) wide. For each child, cut dowel to 17 inches (43 cm). For each child, cut ribbon into a 25-inch (63.5-cm) length.

Measure hook side of Velcro to the ping pong balls, cut to appropriate length. Remove paper and adhere around the center of each ping pong balls (sketch a). Place balls in resealable plastic bag.

## INSTRUCT EACH CHILD IN THE FOLLOWING PROCEDURES:

- Fold the top 2 inches (5 cm) of the large piece of red felt over the dowel rod and glue (sketch b).
- Glue one piece each of blue, green and yellow felt onto the large piece of felt, creating a four-color square (sketch c).
- Thread the ribbon through the eye of a craft needle. Push the needle through the felt at the top of the red felt, under the dowel and about 1-inch (2.5-cm) from the edge. Tie two or three knots. Then push the needle through about 1 inch (2.5 cm) from the opposite edge. Remove needle and tie two or three knots (sketch d).
- Cut Target Words apart. (Optional: Place lengths of clear packing tape over cards and trim tape to edges of cards.) Cut remaining hook side of Velcro into eight pieces, attaching one piece to the back of each word card. Place word cards into resealable plastic bag.
- To play game: Children select four word cards and place one in each section of the felt game board. Hang board on a wall. Stand several feet away and toss ping pong balls at target. In the section in which the most ping pong balls land, name a way a kid can serve others at that place.

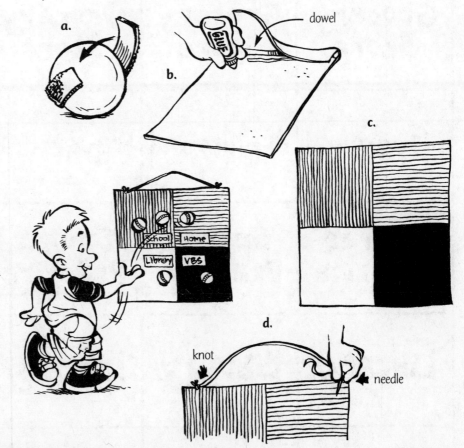

## CONVERSATION

In today's story, two men worked hard for their master and one man hardly worked. Jesus wants us to be like the men who worked hard. Whatever we do, even playing a game, we can do our very best.

Who can tell me the Daily Challenge we're talking about today? Pause for children to respond, "Get Going!" God has made each of us in different ways so that we can meet the different needs of others. When we get going and help others, we show that we love God! So are you ready to Get Going? Encourage children to respond, "Got Going!" Good!

| | | | |
|---|---|---|---|
| School | School | School | School |
| VBS | VBS | VBS | VBS |
| Home | Home | Home | Home |
| Grocery Store | Grocery Store | Grocery Store | Grocery Store |
| Playground | Playground | Playground | Playground |
| Sports Practice | Sports Practice | Sports Practice | Sports Practice |
| Library | Library | Library | Library |
| Friend's House | Friend's House | Friend's House | Friend's House |

# BUTTERFLY ON a STICK (20-30 MINUTES)

## MATERIALS

- Butterfly Patterns (p. 56)
- lightweight cardboard or card stock
- black paint
- blue permanent markers or paint pens

**For every 2 children—**
- 22x28-inch (56x71-cm) black poster board

**For each child—**
- ½-inch (1.3-cm) diameter dowel
- 2 8½x11-inch (21.5x28-cm) transparency sheets
- 5 1-inch (2.5-cm) black pom-poms
- black chenille wire

## STANDARD SUPPLIES

- scissors
- white crayons or colored pencils
- transparent tape
- glue

## PREPARATION

Enlarge Butterfly Patterns at 200 percent, printing on 8½x14-inch (21.5x35.5-cm) paper. Cut out patterns, and then trace them onto lightweight cardboard or card stock and cut out, making one of each pattern for every two or three children. Cut poster board in half, creating one 14-inch (35.5-cm) piece for each child. Paint the dowels black.

## INSTRUCT EACH CHILD IN THE FOLLOWING PROCEDURES:

- Fold piece of poster board in half. Place open end of Wing Frame pattern on the fold. Use white crayon or colored pencil to trace pattern onto poster board and then cut out (sketch a).
- Trace Body pattern on a piece of leftover poster board and cut out (sketch b).
- Use blue permanent marker or paint pen to trace Wing Color Patterns onto both transparency sheets and then color the wings (sketch c). Cut out transparent wings.
- Place transparent wings on black butterfly you prepared. Use pieces of tape to tape the wings in place. Tape all the way around, not leaving any gaps (sketch d).
- Glue butterfly to dowel, body to wings and pom-poms to card-stock body. Bend chenille wire in half, curl the ends of the antennae with your fingers, and glue to card-stock body.

### Simplification Ideas
- Instead of having students trace Wing Color Patterns onto transparency sheets, use sheets that can be photocopied and copy Wing Color Patterns.
- Instead of coloring transparency sheets, use blue sheets of acetate, construction paper or poster board for interior of wings.

### Enrichment Idea
Add glitter to the wings using glitter and glue or glitter glue pens.

a.

fold

b.

c.

d.

# BUTTERFLY PATTERNS
### photocopy at 200%

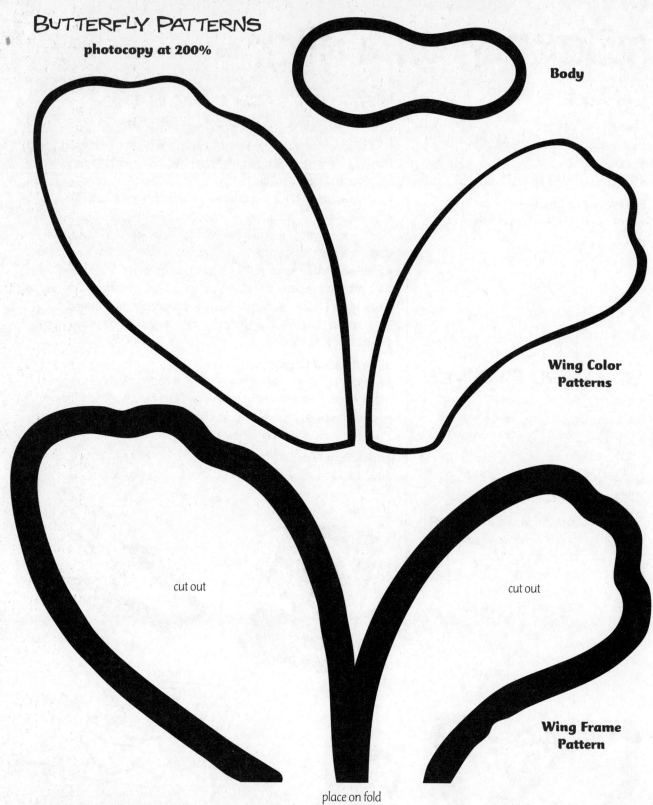

**Body**

**Wing Color Patterns**

cut out

cut out

**Wing Frame Pattern**

place on fold

## CONVERSATION

Butterflies are one of the few animals you'll find in ALL layers of the rainforest, from the forest floor all the way to the emergent layer. They're going all the time! And as they travel through the rainforest, they help pollinate plants and keep the forest lush and beautiful. God wants us to work hard like the butterflies do. In Colossians 3:23, our Bibles say, "Whatever you do, work at it with all your heart, as working for the Lord, not for men."

What is the Daily Challenge for today? Pause for students to respond, "Get Going." God wants us to Get Going and use the talents and abilities He's given us to show our love for Him by serving others. Are you ready to Get Going? Encourage students to respond, "Got Going!" Good!

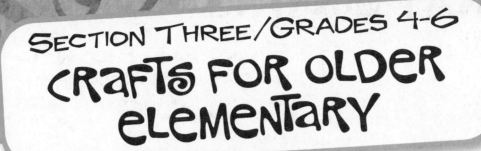

# SECTION THREE/GRADES 4-6
# CRAFTS FOR OLDER ELEMENTARY

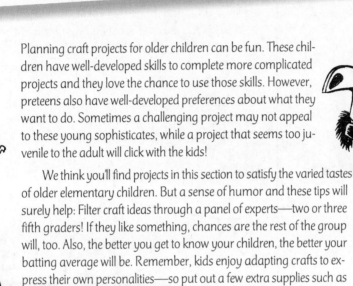

Planning craft projects for older children can be fun. These children have well-developed skills to complete more complicated projects and they love the chance to use those skills. However, preteens also have well-developed preferences about what they want to do. Sometimes a challenging project may not appeal to these young sophisticates, while a project that seems too juvenile to the adult will click with the kids!

We think you'll find projects in this section to satisfy the varied tastes of older elementary children. But a sense of humor and these tips will surely help: Filter craft ideas through a panel of experts—two or three fifth graders! If they like something, chances are the rest of the group will, too. Also, the better you get to know your children, the better your batting average will be. Remember, kids enjoy adapting crafts to express their own personalities—so put out a few extra supplies such as wiggle eyes, glitter glue, and fabric or paper scraps. You just might be surprised at what they dream up!

# GLITTERY GROWING BOWL (20-30 MINUTES)

## MATERIALS

- water
- small bowls
- variety of tissue paper, particularly shades of blue
- iridescent glitter

**For each child—**
- glass ivy bowl
- water plant (available at nurseries and pet stores that carry aquarium supplies)

**Optional—**
- craft punches (shaped like flowers, leaves, bugs, frogs, lizards, etc.)

## STANDARD SUPPLIES

- newspaper
- white glue
- scissors
- foam paintbrushes

## PREPARATION

Cover tables with newspaper. In small bowls, place a mixture of equal parts white glue and water. Prepare a bowl for every two or three children.

## CONVERSATION

**The bowls we made today help plants grow in water. But in our Bible story today, we heard about different kinds of soil and how plants can only grow in good soil. God wants us to be like the good soil. He wants us to listen to and put into action the good things He tells us to do in His Word, the Bible.**

**Who can tell me the Daily Challenge we're talking about today?** Pause for children to respond, "Get It." **When we say we've Got It, we mean that we heard, understand and will do what the Bible tells us to do. So do you Get It?** Encourage children to respond, "Got it!" **Good!**

## INSTRUCT EACH CHILD IN THE FOLLOWING PROCEDURES:

- Cut or tear blue tissue paper into small squares (sketch a). Cut flowers, leaves, bugs, frogs, lizards, etc. out of the other colors of tissue paper. (Optional: Use craft punches to punch shapes.)
- Paint a small area of the bowl with glue. Place tissue-paper pieces over the glue, overlapping the pieces slightly. Use several different shades of blue (sketch b). Continue until the bottom half of the bowl is covered with tissue, leaving the top half of the bowl clear.
- Paint another coat of glue over the tissue paper and then decorate with shapes you cut from tissue paper (sketch c).
- Paint another coat of glue over the tissue paper and sprinkle with iridescent glitter (sketch d).
- When glue is dry, pour water into the bowl, filling half full. Float a plant on the water.

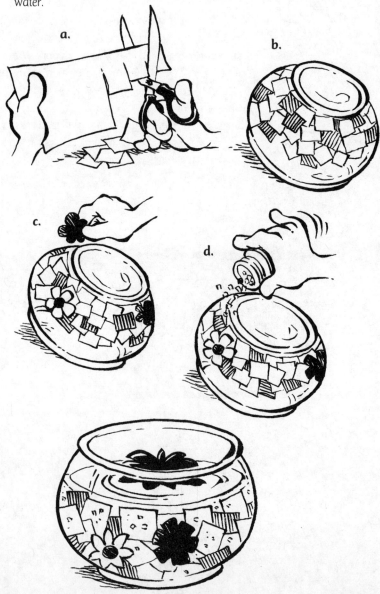

# MeGa Rain Sticks (20-30 MINUTES)

## MATERIALS

- ¾-inch (1.9-cm) nails
- spoons
- rice
- beans
- variety of decorative paper (tissue paper, wallpaper scraps, scrapbook paper, construction paper, etc.)
- clear Con-Tact paper
- ¼-inch (0.6-cm) ribbon or plastic lacing
- pony beads
- variety of brightly colored duct tape

**For each child—**
- cardboard mailing tube with end caps

## STANDARD SUPPLIES

- hammers
- craft glue
- scissors
- transparent tape

## INSTRUCT EACH CHILD IN THE FOLLOWING PROCEDURES:

- Hammer 10-12 nails into the mailing tube in a random fashion (sketch a).
- Glue one end cap onto one end of the mailing tube. Place two or three spoonfuls each of rice and beans into the tube and glue remaining end cap on other end of the tube.
- Cut decorative paper into squares and other shapes. Cut a piece of clear Con-Tact paper large enough to wrap around tube with a slight overlap. Remove backing from Con-Tact paper and place Con-Tact paper sticky side up on table.
- Place decorative paper pieces on to sticky side of Con-Tact paper, creating stripes, flowers, etc. (sketch b). Leave open space between the paper pieces so that the Con-Tact paper will stick to your tube.
- Wrap the decorated Con-Tact paper onto the tube (sketch c). If needed, use transparent tape to secure.
- Measure ribbon or plastic lacing from your nose to the end of your fingers (sketch d) and cut. Repeat so that you have two or three lengths of ribbon or lacing.
- Place ribbon or lacing across a length of duct tape (sketch e). Wrap tape around the end of your rain stick.
- String beads onto the ribbon or plastic lacing, tying knots to secure (sketch f).

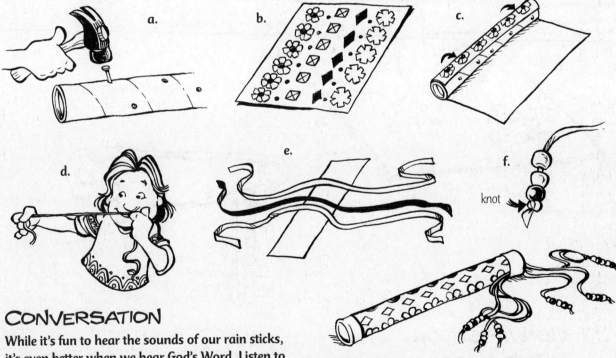

a. b. c. d. e. f. knot

## CONVERSATION

While it's fun to hear the sounds of our rain sticks, it's even better when we hear God's Word. Listen to Psalm 119:11: "I have hidden your word in my heart that I might not sin against you." God's Word is the Bible, and hiding it in our hearts means that we read, remember, love and obey God's Word.

What is the Daily Challenge for today? Pause for children to respond, "Get It!" **Living according to God's Word is the BEST way to live. When we hide God's Word in our heart and show it by the way we live, then we show that we "Get It." Get it?** Encourage children to respond, "Got it!" **Good!**

# BeaDeD Sheep PiNS (20-30 MINUTES)

## MATERIALS

- Beaded Sheep Pin Patterns (p. 61)
- seed beads (white, black, green, etc.)
- bowls
- crayons or colored pencils

**For each child—**
- 15 1¹⁄₁₆-inch (2.7-cm) safety pins
- 2-inch (5-cm) safety pin
- felt square

## PREPARATION

For each child, photocopy Beaded Sheep Pin Patterns. Pour some of each color of seed beads into a separate bowl. Prepare a bowl of seed beads in each color for every three or four children. Place different sizes of safety pins in separate bowls.

## INSTRUCT EACH CHILD IN THE FOLLOWING PROCEDURES:

- Choose a pattern or design your own using crayons or colored pencils and the blank pattern. Decide the colors of seed beads you need for your pattern. Pinch some seed beads of each color and place on your felt square (sketch a).
- Select 14 small safety pins and one of the large safety pins. Each column in the pattern represents one of the smaller seed beads. Starting at the top of column 1 and moving down, place the color of bead indicated on a small safety pin. Close pin and place on large safety pin (sketch b).
- Repeat for columns 2-14. Close large safety pin. Use your last small pin to fasten your beaded sheep pin to your clothes, backpack, or wherever you want!

### Enrichment Ideas
- Attach lengths of plastic or leather lacing to either end of the large safety pin to turn it into a necklace.
- Use a dowel, yarn and pony beads to create a larger beaded wall hanging. Follow the pattern, stringing pony beads on knotted lengths of yarn and tying each to a dowel. Tie a length of yarn on either end of dowel to form a hanger.

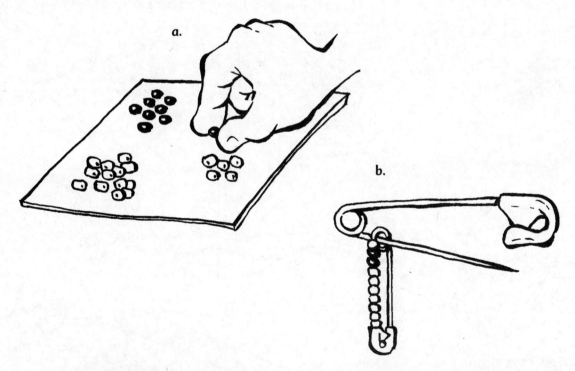

a.

b.

## CONVERSATION

**Our beaded sheep pins can remind us that without Jesus as our Savior, each of us is lost like the sheep in today's story. We all do wrong things and need His gift of forgiveness.** **Who can tell me the Daily Challenge we're talking about today?** Pause for children to respond, "Get Found!" **Without Jesus, we're like lost sheep. But once we believe in Jesus as our Savior and become members of God's family, we can say that we've been found!**

# Beaded Sheep Pin Patterns

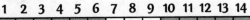

**COLOR KEY**
Green 🔲
Black ⬛
White ⬜

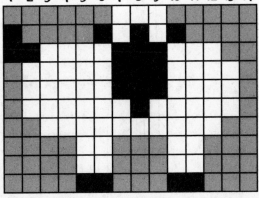

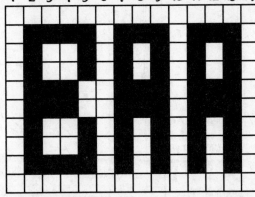

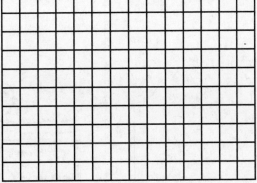

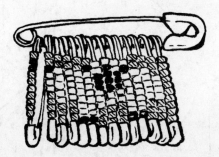

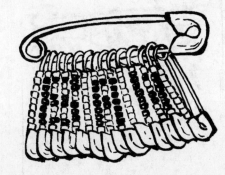

# OJOS De DiOs (20-25 MINUTES)

## MATERIALS

• sticks gathered from trees
• variety of yarn

## STANDARD SUPPLIES

• measuring sticks
• scissors

## INSTRUCT EACH CHILD IN THE FOLLOWING PROCEDURES:

• Select a long stick about 30 inches (76 cm) long; a shorter stick about 20 inches (51 cm) long; and three smaller sticks, each about 7 inches (18 cm) long (sketch a). Use a measuring stick to break sticks to the appropriate sizes.

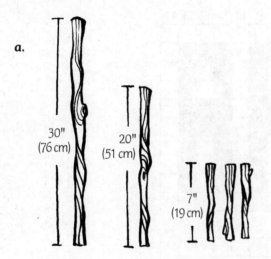

a.

30"
(76 cm)

20"
(51 cm)

7"
(19 cm)

• Choose a color of yarn for the middle of the eye, measure from your nose to the end of your fingers and cut yarn (sketch b).

b.

• Using the two longest sticks, make a cross. With one end of the yarn, tie the cross in place, wrapping diagonally in one direction, then the other, and finally tying a knot to secure the yarn (sketch c).

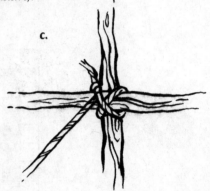

c.

• Beginning with yarn in the lower left of the cross, wind the yarn under the lower center stick, over the top to the top of the left-hand stick. Wrap under that stick and up to the stick at the top, turning the sticks in your hand as you work. Continue wrapping around and around, holding yarn fairly tight as you wind (sketches d and e).

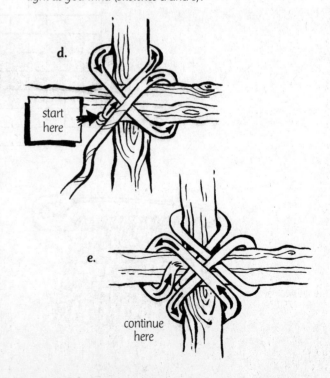

d.

start here

e.

continue here

- Continue wrapping until you wish to change colors. Cut another length of yarn in the new color, knot it on to the yarn you are using, cut off any extra of the first color and continue the wrapping pattern with the new color (sketch f).

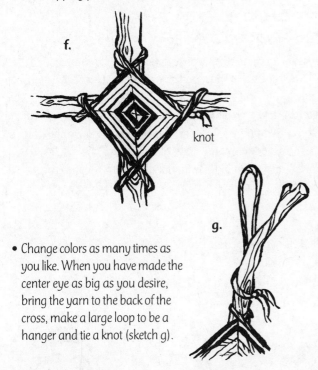

f.

knot

g.

- Change colors as many times as you like. When you have made the center eye as big as you desire, bring the yarn to the back of the cross, make a large loop to be a hanger and tie a knot (sketch g).

- Add smaller crosses, one on either side of the first cross, by adding one of the small sticks to the cross bar. Use the same wrapping pattern, and change colors as desired. Once the cross is as big as you want, wrap the yarn around the stick, moving towards the center eye. Tie a knot when you reach the center eye. Create another small cross on the other side of the center cross. Repeat the wrapping (sketch h).

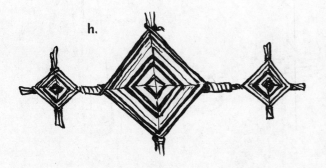

h.

- Add another smaller cross midway to the bottom of the cross. Tie a knot around the stick when you have reached the desired size (sketch i).

i.

- To create the hanging pompoms, wrap yarn around three fingers 13 times. Pull the looped yarn off your fingers and tie another piece of yarn around the middle of the yarn loop. Tie tightly with two knots (sketch j). Cut the loops at the bottom of the pom-pom. Tie onto the Ojo de Dios below the three smaller crosses.

j.

### Simplification Ideas
- Use dowels, precut to the appropriate sizes.
- Use one color of yarn for each Ojo de Dios.

### Enrichment Idea
Provide beads and feathers for children to add more decoration to their Ojos de Dios. Tie on additional lengths of yarn on which to string beads. Feathers can be added by tying knots around the stem of the feather.

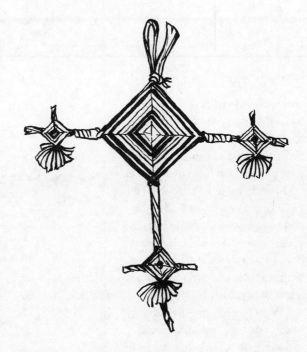

## CONVERSATION

Today's project is a traditional South American craft called *Ojos de Dios,* which means "God's Eyes." We had to make several crosses. These crosses can remind us that Jesus died on a cross because He loves us. In John 3:16, the Bible tells us, "For God so loved the world that he gave his one and only Son, that whoever believes in him shall not perish but have eternal life." When Jesus died and rose again, He made it possible for us to live with Him forever!

What is the Daily Challenge for today? Pause for children to respond, "Get Found!" Without Jesus as our Savior, it's like we're lost and alone. But when we become members of God's family, we can say that we got found!

# WALKING STICK (25-30 MINUTES)

## MATERIALS

- tape in a variety of colors and widths (masking tape, electrical tape, packing tape, duct tape, etc.)
- permanent markers or paint pens
- twine
- wooden beads

**For each child—**
- 1-inch (2.5-cm) wooden dowel, 4 feet (1.2 m) long

## STANDARD SUPPLIES

- scissors
- measuring sticks

## INSTRUCT EACH CHILD IN THE FOLLOWING PROCEDURES:

- Choose two or three types of tape and cut into pieces long enough to wrap around the dowel. Apply tape to dowel, either following a pattern or creating a random design (sketch a).
- Decorate spaces between the tape with permanent markers or paint pens (sketch b).
- Cut twine into two or three 18- to 20-inch (45.5- to 51-cm) lengths. Place lengths of twine next to each other across one or more lengths of tape (sketch c).
- Wrap tape around dowel, leaving strands of twine dangling from both sides of the tape. String wooden beads onto each length of twine and tie with several knots (sketch d).

**Simplification Idea**
Use only permanent markers or paint pens to decorate the dowels.

**Enrichment Idea**
Use stain and/or acrylic paint to create designs on the walking stick.

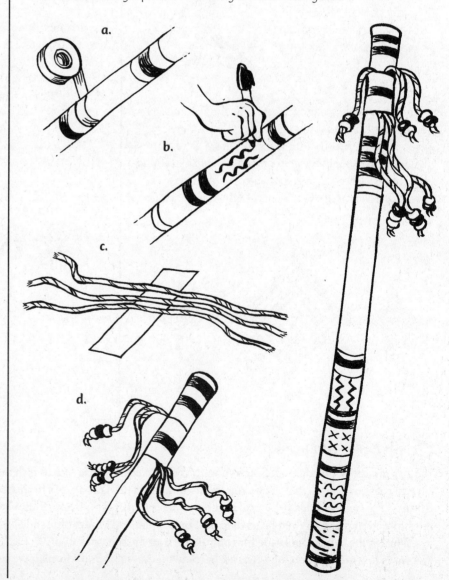

a.

b.

c.

d.

## CONVERSATION

Our walking sticks can remind us of the man who was walking to Jericho in today's Bible story. Jesus told this parable to explain that just as God has shown love by inviting us to be a part of His family, we can obey God by showing love and giving help to all people—even when it means doing something we don't like or helping someone who isn't popular with our friends.

Who can tell me the Daily Challenge we're talking about today? Pause for children to respond, "Get God's Love!" God's love is so amazing, once we get it, we want to share that love with others! So are you ready to Get God's Love and help others? Encourage children to respond, "Got God's Love!" Good!

# TALENT NECKLACE (20-30 MINUTES)

## MATERIALS

- magazines (children's magazines, toy catalogs, etc.)
- variety of card stock
- clear packing tape

**For each child—**
- 5 or 6 split rings (available at hardware stores or where jewelry supplies are sold)
- 24-inch (61-cm) length ball chain and connector (available at hardware stores)

**Optional—**
- scrap paper, stickers (SonQuest Stickers available from Gospel Light)

## STANDARD SUPPLIES

- measuring stick
- scissors
- glue sticks
- hole punch
- pencils

## CONVERSATION

**Our necklaces remind us of some of the things we're good at doing. Whatever we are doing—whether playing a game, playing music, reading, helping others—we can do our very best. Just like two of the servants in today's story did their best with the money their master had given them.**

**Who can tell me the Daily Challenge we're talking about today?** Pause for children to respond, "Get Going!" **God has made each of us in different ways so that we can meet the different needs of others. When we get going and help others, we show that we love God! So are you ready to Get Going?** Encourage children to respond, "Got Going!" **Good!**

## INSTRUCT EACH CHILD IN THE FOLLOWING PROCEDURES:

- Look through magazines and/or catalogs to find words or pictures to represent some of your talents or abilities. Make sure they are 2 inches (5 cm) or smaller. Cut them out.
- Use glue stick to glue words or pictures on pieces of card stock (sketch a). You may use one or more colors of card stock. (Optional: Draw pictures or write words you would like on your necklace. Place pictures, words or stickers on pieces of card stock.)
- Cover card stock with a piece of clear packing tape (sketch b). Then flip over and cover that side with a piece of clear packing tape.
- Cut out each picture to make individual charms to go on your necklace. Punch a hole near the top of each charm (sketch c).
- Thread a split ring through the hole in each charm (sketch d).
- Thread charms onto ball chain and secure connector.

### Budget Idea

Instead of ball chain, use leather lacing or plastic lacing for necklaces.

a.

b.

c.

d.

# RAiNFOReST PaPeR HOLDeR

## (25-35 MINUTES)

## MATERIALS

- Snake, Gecko and Butterfly Patterns from Rainforest Animals Patterns (p. 31)
- Rainforest Leaf Pattern (p. 68)
- Large and Small Flower Patterns (p. 68)
- Palm Tree Patterns (p. 68)
- ⅛-inch (0.3-cm) craft wood
- saw (hand saw, jigsaw, circular saw, miter saw, etc.)
- green paint
- variety of craft foam, including brown and several shades of green
- glitter glue

**For each child—**
- 2 12-mm wiggle eyes
- spring-type clothespin

## STANDARD SUPPLIES

- white card stock
- ruler
- paintbrushes
- scissors
- pencils
- craft glue
- hole punch

## CONVERSATION

**Our paper holders can hold letters, homework assignments or other important papers we don't want to lose. What is the Daily Challenge for today?** Pause for children to respond, "Get Found!" **When we talk about "Get(ting) Found," we're talking about becoming a member of God's family. God sent Jesus to Earth because He loves us! When Jesus died and rose again, He made it possible for us to join God's family and live with Him forever.**

In John 3:16 the Bible says, "For God so loved the world that he gave his one and only Son, that whoever believes in him shall not perish but have eternal life." **God wants each of us to Get Found and become a member of His family. So how about it? Did anyone here Get Found?** Willing children respond, "Got found!" **Good!**

## PREPARATION

Cover tables with newspaper. Photocopy Rainforest Leaves Pattern, Flower Patterns, Palm Tree Patterns, Snake, Gecko and Butterfly Patterns onto card stock, making a copy of each for every two or three children.

For each child, use saw to cut wood into a 4x12-inch (10x30.5-cm) piece. Then, mark 6 inches (15 cm) on one side of the piece of wood and 7½ (19 cm) inches on the other. Draw a line between the two marks and cut on line (sketch a), making two angled pieces (sketch a). Paint front, back and edges of the wood pieces.

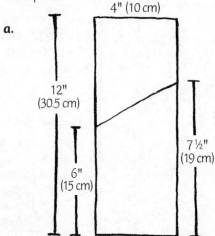

a.

4" (10 cm)

12" (30.5 cm)

6" (15 cm)

7½" (19 cm)

## INSTRUCT EACH CHILD IN THE FOLLOWING PROCEDURES:

- Cut out patterns from card stock. Use pencils to trace four or five leaves and Palm Tree Top onto sheets of green craft foam. Trace Palm Tree Trunk onto brown craft foam. Choose a snake, butterfly or gecko pattern as well as one or two flower patterns and trace onto your choice of colored craft foam (sketch b). Cut out shapes.

b.

**Timesaver Tip:** Before class, cut out patterns from card stock.

- Place each wood piece so that the taller edge is on the outside. Use glitter glue to make stripes, decorating the front of each wood piece (sketch c).

c.

- Use glitter glue to create veins in the leaves and add dimension to the Palm Tree Trunk and Top (sketch d).

d.

- Glue top of palm tree to trunk and then glue to the taller wood piece. Glue leaves and one or more flowers below and to the right of the tree (sketch e).

e.

- Glue leaves and animal to the front of the paper holder. Add wiggle eyes to animal.

- Use a hole punch to create dots to decorate the gecko. Glue dots on the gecko (sketch f).

f.

- Under adult supervision, use glue gun to glue the clothespin 1½ inches (4 cm) from the left side of the back piece of wood (sketch g). Off set the front piece of wood by moving it to the left approximately 1½ inches (4 cm). Glue to the other side of the clothespin.

g.

**Simplification Idea**
Provide foam die-cuts of leaves and animals (available at craft stores).

**Enrichment Idea**
Provide other animal patterns. Children decorate paper holders with their favorite rainforest animal.

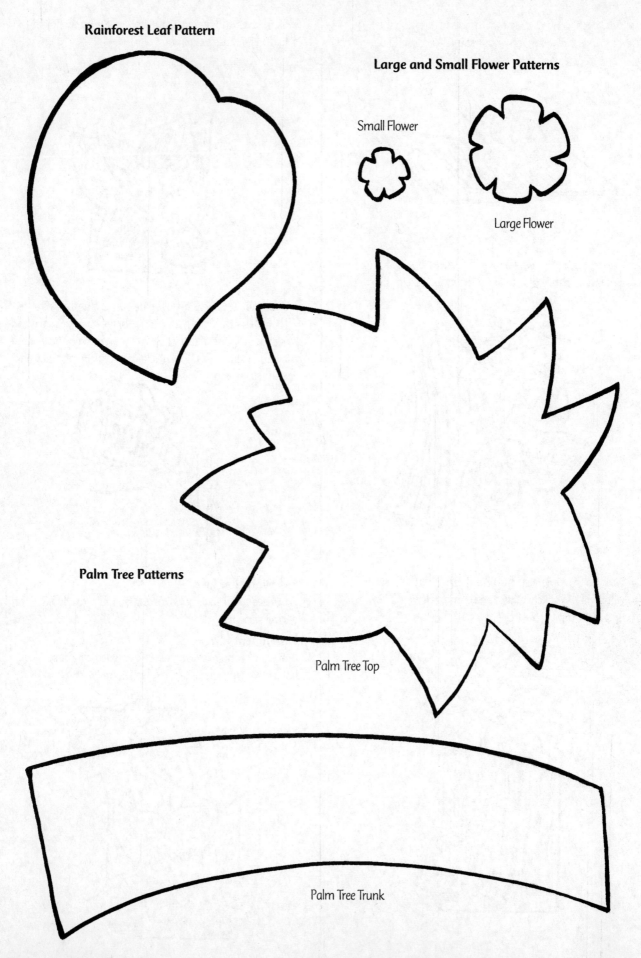

**Rainforest Leaf Pattern**

**Large and Small Flower Patterns**

Small Flower

Large Flower

**Palm Tree Patterns**

Palm Tree Top

Palm Tree Trunk

# FaUX STaiNeD GLaSS (20-30 MINUTES)

## MATERIALS
- Stained Glass Patterns (p. 71)
- aluminum foil
- electrical tape
- ribbon
- variety of permanent markers or paint pens

**For each child—**
- 8½x11-inch (21.5x28-cm) transparency sheet

## STANDARD SUPPLIES
- transparent tape
- scissors
- hole punch

## PREPARATION
For each child, photocopy or print Stained Glass Pattern onto a transparency sheet. For each child, cut foil into a 9x12-inch (23x30.5-cm) piece.

**Note:** Be sure to use transparency sheets specially designed to be used in a photocopier or printer.

**Budget Option:** Instead of using transparency sheets that can be sent through a printer or photocopier, use regular transparency sheets. Photocopy pattern onto a sheet of paper. Children place patterns under transparency sheets and trace it, using a black permanent marker or paint pen.

## INSTRUCT EACH CHILD IN THE FOLLOWING PROCEDURES:

- Place transparency so that the printed side is facedown. (Coloring on the same side that was printed on can cause the ink to be removed.) Color each section of the transparency, using a variety of colors (sketch a). Set aside to dry.

a.

- Crumple foil and then carefully flatten it out, trying not to tear foil (sketch b).

b.

- Place the transparency over the foil, line up the left edges and tape together. Fold the transparent tape over the edge to secure both layers. Trim excess foil from other edges and tape them (sketch c).

c.

• Using black electrical tape, fold tape over one edge of the stained glass design. Tape remaining edges (sketch d).

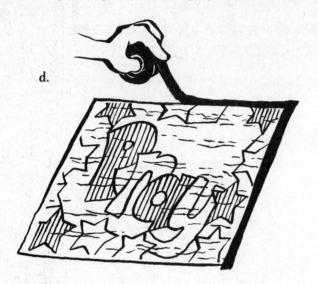

d.

• Use hole punch to make holes near the top corners (sketch e). Cut an 18-inch (45.5-cm) length of ribbon. Tie a knot around one of the holes thread through ribbon through other hole, tying a second knot to create a hanger for the stained glass.

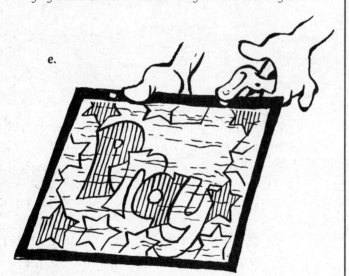

e.

## Simplification Idea

Make a sun catcher. Don't use foil. Instead, hang colored transparencies in a window and let the light shine through the design.

## Enrichment Ideas

• Children use sheets of paper to draw their own stained glass designs, place designs under transparency sheets and trace, using a black permanent marker or paint pen. Children complete design as described above.

• Add adhesive-backed craft foam shapes (stars, flowers, cross, etc.). Peel paper from adhesive backing and stick the shapes around the edge of the stained glass or sandwich ribbon between two shapes.

## CONVERSATION

**Our stained glass designs remind us to pray. Jesus wants all of us to know that we can trust God to love and help us when we ask Him! No matter where we are or what we are doing, we can pray to God. He will hear our prayers and help us.**

**Who can tell me the Daily Challenge we're talking about today?** Pause for children to respond, "Get Praying!" **When we need something or are feeling sad, angry or scared, the best thing we can do is talk to God. Because we can pray to God about anything, at any time, we can always have peace. Having peace means we know that whatever happens, God is with us, that God is good and He provides what we need. So are you ready to Get Praying?** Encourage children to respond, "Got Praying!" **Good!**

# STAINED GLASS PATTERNS

**Note:** Enlarge patterns 155% to fill 8½x11 sheet.

# Toucan Wind Chime (30-40 MINUTES)

## MATERIALS

- Toucan Patterns (p. 74)
- black acrylic paint
- black, white and yellow craft foam
- black feathers
- variety of black satin ribbon
- ¼-inch (0.6-cm) wooden dowels

**For each child—**
- 6-inch (15-cm) terra cotta pot
- 2 15-mm wiggle eyes
- 3 jingle bells

## STANDARD SUPPLIES

- paintbrushes
- white card stock
- pencils
- white colored crayons or pencils
- scissors
- low-temperature glue gun

## PREPARATION

Paint the terra cotta pots black. For each child, photocopy Toucan Patterns onto card stock. Cut the dowel into two ¾-inch (7.1-cm) pieces.

## INSTRUCT EACH CHILD IN THE FOLLOWING PROCEDURES:

- Cut out Toucan Patterns. Use a pencil to trace the tummy onto white craft foam, and two beaks and two eyes on yellow craft foam. Use a white crayon or colored pencil to trace the tail, two wings and two beak details onto black craft foam (sketch a). Cut out all shapes.

a.

- Align the two beak pieces and with adult help, use glue gun to glue the top edges together (sketch b). Then spread apart the lower corners and glue to the top of the tummy (sketch c).

glue along dotted line

b.

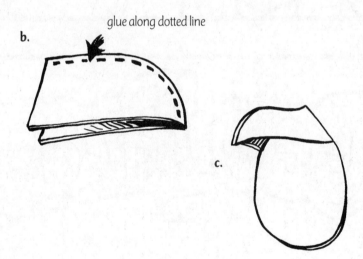

c.

## CONVERSATION

**Our wind chimes can remind us to pray to God. Toucans are loud noisy birds that call out to each other. God wants us to call out to Him—wherever we are, whatever we are doing! Philippians 4:6-7 is a favorite verse for many people. It says, "Do not be anxious about anything, but in everything, by prayer and petition, with thanksgiving, present your requests to God. And the peace of God . . . will guard your hearts and your minds in Christ Jesus."**

**When times are difficult, it's good to remember that God always listens to our prayers, and we can always have His peace by trusting in Him. What is the Daily Challenge for today?** Pause for children to respond, "Get Praying." **Whatever happens, we can trust God and not worry! So how about it? Are you ready to Get Praying?** Encourage children to respond, "Got Praying!" **Good!**

- With adult help, use glue gun to glue feathers to one side of each wing and to both sides of the tail (sketch d).

d.

- With adult help, use glue gun to glue tummy onto terra cotta pot (sketch e).

e.

- Glue beak details to the ends of the beak (sketch f). Glue eye pieces next to beak and glue on wiggle eyes (sketch g).

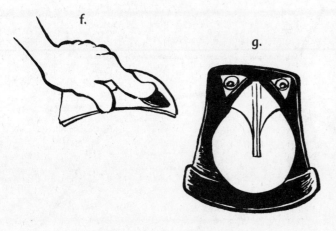

f.

g.

- Glue wings on either side of the pot and the tail to the back (sketch h).

h.

- Tie ribbons onto the dowel, leaving a 12-inch long loop at the top of the dowel. Add ribbons of varying widths to the dowel (sketch i). Thread the top loop through the opening of the pot. Glue into place.

i.

- Hang the bird on a hanger. Tie jingle bells at varying lengths to the ribbons dangling from the center of the bird.

## Simplification Ideas

- Instead of using glue gun, use glue dots. Glue dots are available in the scrapbooking section of most craft stores.
- Rather than craft-foam pieces, glue feathers onto the pot. Use permanent markers or paint pens to add details to the beak and body of the toucan. You can use white-out correction pens or acrylic paint to make the tummy, instead of using white craft foam.
- Use inexpensive black plastic pots from a nursery. If needed, you can use an awl and hammer to punch a hole in the center bottom to thread ribbon through.

## Enrichment Idea

Create a variety of rainforest birds using different colors of paint, craft foam and feathers.

# Toucan Patterns

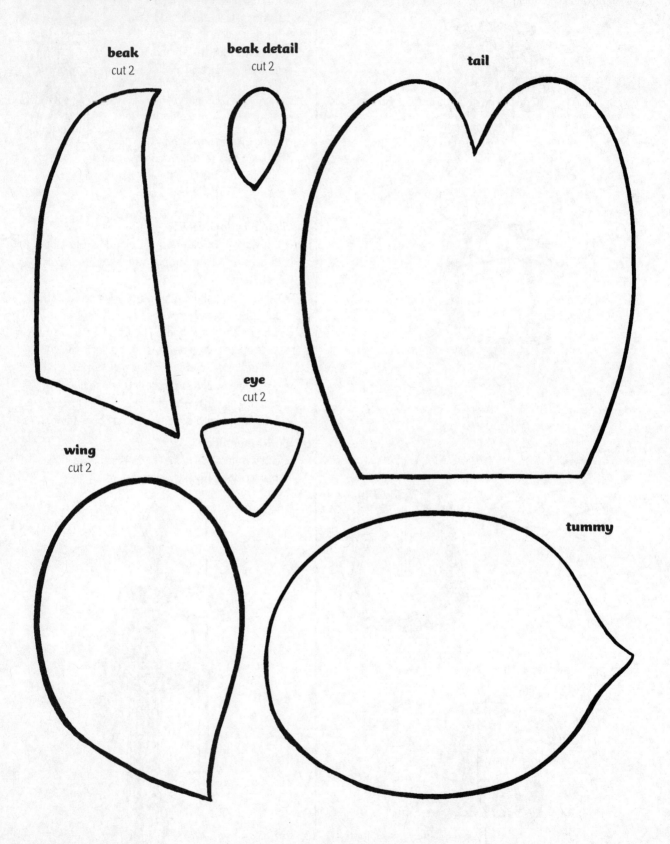

beak
cut 2

beak detail
cut 2

tail

eye
cut 2

wing
cut 2

tummy

# JUNGLE VINE (30-40 MINUTES)

## MATERIALS

- Snake, Gecko and Butterfly Patterns from Rainforest Animals Patterns (p. 31)
- Monkey Patterns (p. 77)
- Vine Patterns (p. 78)
- Frog Patterns (p. 79)
- garden wire (green plastic-coated wire)
- wire cutters
- variety of craft foam including different shades of green, black, white, tan, red, blue, etc.
- green chenille wires
- ribbon
- permanent markers

## STANDARD SUPPLIES

- card stock
- measuring stick
- scissors
- white crayons or colored pencils
- pencils
- white glue

## PREPARATION

Enlarge Snake, Gecko and Butterfly Patterns on photocopier so that butterfly is approximately 6 inches (15 cm) across and snake and gecko are each approximately 9½ inches (24 cm) long. Photocopy patterns onto card stock, making one for every two or three children. Also photocopy Monkey Patterns, Frog Patterns and Vine Patterns onto card stock, making one for every two or three children. For each child, use wire cutters to cut a 3-foot (0.9-m) length of garden wire.

## CONVERSATION

Our jungle vines can help us remember some of the wonderful things we've learned about God at SonQuest Rainforest. Everyone worked hard to make his or her vine. Our Bibles tell us God is pleased when we work hard. In Colossians 3:23, our Bibles say, "Whatever you do, work at it with all your heart, as working for the Lord, not for men." When we are working for the Lord, it means we are trying to do our best work. When we use our abilities to serve others, we ARE working for God! We're showing that we love God.

What is the Daily Challenge for today? Pause for children to respond, "Get Going." One of the animals in the jungle vines we made is a butterfly. As butterflies travel through the rainforest, they pollinate plants and help keep the forest lush and beautiful. God wants us to use the talents and abilities He's given us to show our love for Him by serving others. So how about it? Are you ready to Get Going? Encourage children to respond, "Got Going!" Good!

# INSTRUCT EACH CHILD IN THE FOLLOWING PROCEDURES:

- Cut out patterns as needed. Trace leaf pattern onto several shades of green craft foam, making approximately 15 leaves (sketch a). Trace monkey and butterfly on black (using white crayon or colored pencil), monkey face on tan, monkey mane on white, frog body on red and frog legs on blue. Trace snake, gecko and flower patterns onto colors of craft foam of your own choosing. Cut out pieces.

a.

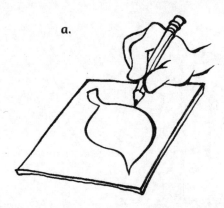

- Glue the animal pieces together: Monkey face and mane onto monkey body, frog legs onto frog. Cut pieces of blue craft foam to decorate butterfly wings (sketch b). You may also decorate snake and gecko with craft-foam scraps.

b.

- Begin lacing the leaves, animals and flowers onto the wire by gently pushing the wire through the craft foam, up through one end of the design and then down through the other end. Add another leaf, large flower or animal (sketch c). Continue until you have filled your wire. If necessary, cut more leaves and/or animals from craft foam.

c.

- Fold a chenille wire over the vine and twist to secure. Wrap the ends of the chenille wire around the pencil to create a spiral and pull on spiral to loosen it. Add as many pipe cleaners as you wish (sketch d).

d.

- Twist the gardening wire several times around a pencil, securing the top and bottom of the vine. Tie a ribbon to the top as a hanger.

- Glue extra flowers onto the leaves to create a colorful jungle vine. Use markers to draw eyes or add other details.

## Simplification Ideas

- Enlarge Leaf Pattern so fewer leaves are needed to cover the wire.
- Purchase a die to cut out leaves and flowers. Or purchase craft-foam die-cuts in leaf and flower shapes.
- Instead of using craft foam, photocopy patterns onto card stock. Children color the card-stock pieces with markers and/or crayons before stringing on garden wire.

# MONKEY PATTERNS

monkey mane

monkey head

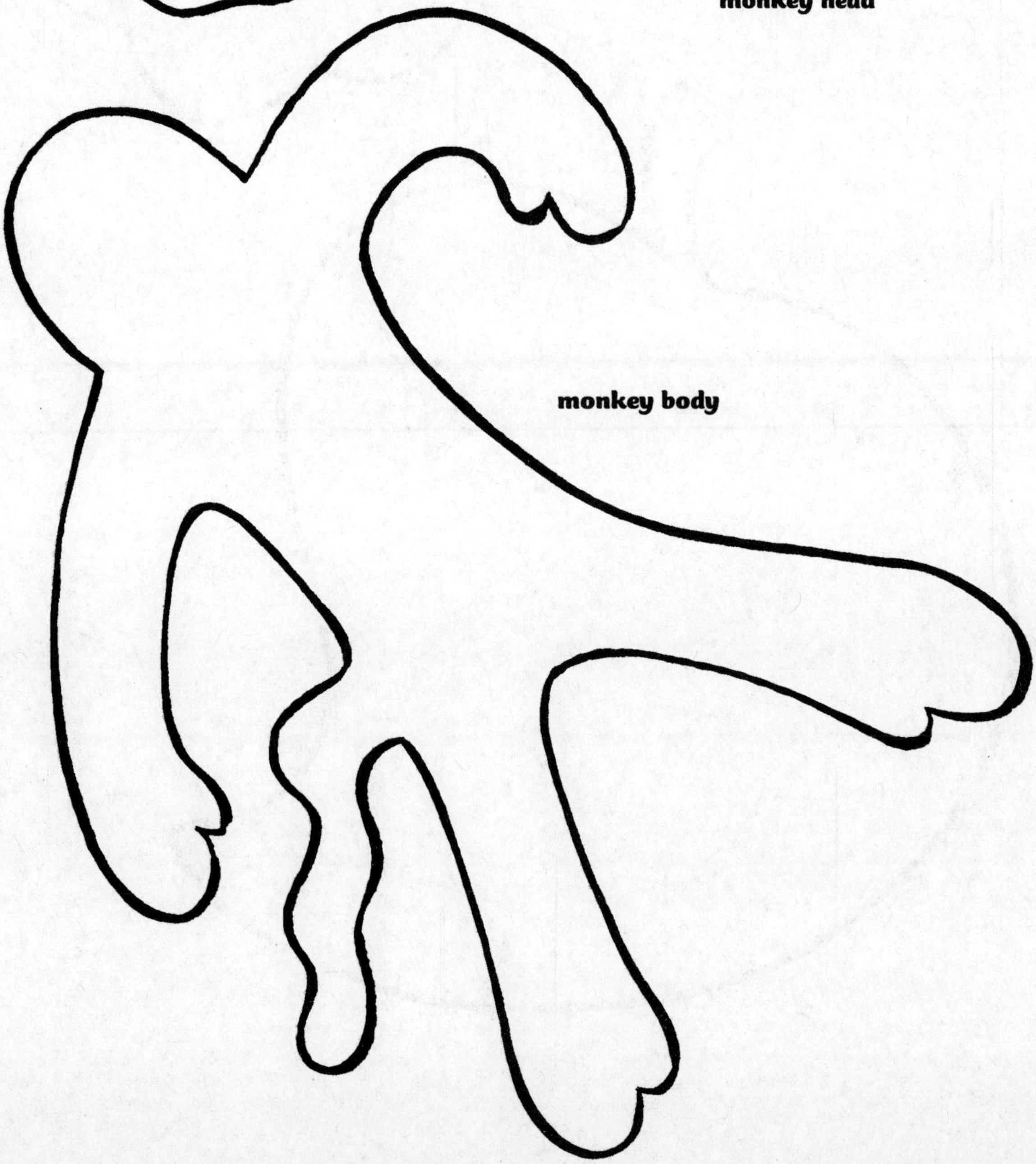

monkey body

**flowers**

leaf

# FROG PATTERNS

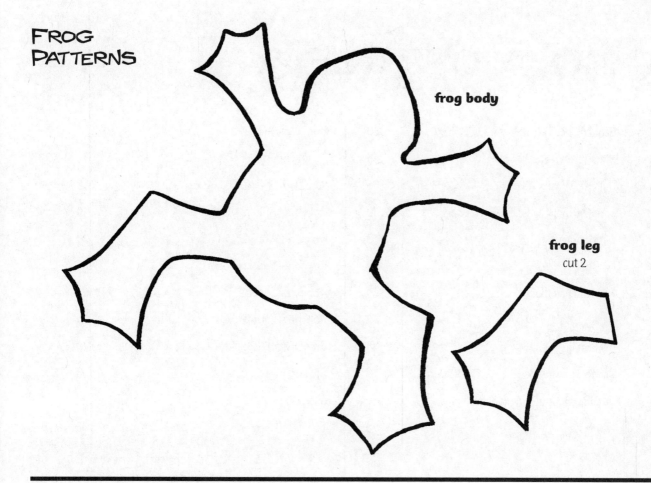

**frog body**

**frog leg**
cut 2

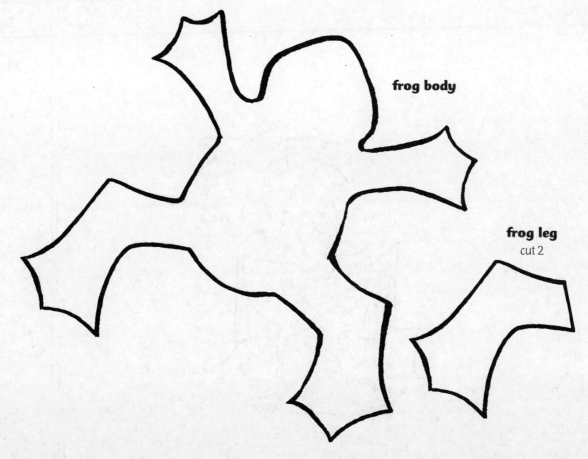

**frog body**

**frog leg**
cut 2

# iNDeX OF CRaFTS